THE FORWARD IMPULSE

TOR DI QUINTO—1906. *The last year that the slide was negotiated sitting back.*

Frontispiece

THE FORWARD IMPULSE

BY PIERO SANTINI
CAPTAIN, ITALIAN CAVALRY RESERVE

Author of *Riding Reflections,* and *Learning to Ride*

ILLUSTRATED WITH
PHOTOGRAPHS AND WITH
SKETCHES BY PAUL BROWN

Xenophon Press

Edition cover and interior © 2016 by Xenophon Press.

All rights reserved. No part of this work may be reproduced or transmitted in any form or by any means, electronic or mechanical, including photocopying, or by any information storage or retrieval system except by a written permission from the publisher.

Published by Xenophon Press
7518 Bayside Road, Franktown, Virginia 23354-2106, U.S.A.

Print ISBN-10: 0-933316-87-9
Print ISBN-13: 978-0-933316-87-4

eBook ISBN-10: 0-933316-89-5
eBook ISBN-13: 978-0-933316-89-8

Cover design by Naia E. Poyer.
Typeset in Times New Roman by Xenophon Press.

Acknowledgement is made to the following for use of photographs reproduced in this book:
Freudy Photos, Inc., Rotofotos, Inc., Edwin Levick, Inc., and Keystone View Co., Inc., of New York; S. Wells Chilson of Birmingham, N.C.; Sport and General, Daily Mirror, Central Press and W.A. Rouch of London, England; d'Amico and Lucchesi of Rome, Italy, and Vianello of San Remo, Italy.
Acknowledgement is made to Paul Brown for the many illustrations reproduced in this book.

Previous print edition published by Hazell, Watson and Viney Ltd., London and Aylesbury. Original printing 1937 by Hazell, Watson and Viney Ltd.

CONTENTS

EDITOR'S PREFACE..i

PREFACE..iii

ILLUSTRATIONS...v

CHAPTER

I. THE FORWARD IMPULSE—1897-1907—The Italian Method versus The High School—The Olympic Games—On Natural Attitudes—On the Horizontal Hand—Contact and Gravity—Reins..1

II. THE STIRRUP—On Mounting and Dismounting, with and without—The Foot and the Stirrup—Foot, Boot and Iron—On Stirrup Accidents 41

III. CROSS-COUNTRY ON ITALIAN PRINCIPLES—On-Misconceptions and Definitions—Constraint vs. Comfort—"Lightening the Forehand"—On Mannerisms 51

IV. THE FLAT—Its Teachings—School for Jockeys 67

V. POLO AND THE ITALIAN METHOD—Leslie Cheape—Polo in Italy—Defects and Remedies—Polo of the Future...............73

VI. THE FORWARD SIDE-SADDLE 87

VII. ON STYLE, BEAUTY AND TAILORS 95

APPENDIX A 99

APPENDIX B 107

XENOPHON PRESS LIBRARY 109

Editor's Preface

What do today's riders want? Safety, horses in perfect unity with their riders, gracious leadership over their mounts, excitement, and movement that qualifies the horses' gaits as works of art.

To achieve these goals, riders must be the custodians of their horses' roundness. Not just remedial neck roundness, but roundness the comes from true engagement of the horse's haunches, roundness that vibrates and slithers through the horses back via the influence of the rider's seat, and energy that softly rounds the neck and terminates in light and willing contact with the bit.

Riders of today must understand the source of this energy is the haunches, and that it is the rider's responsibility to augment and control this energy.

The great master Piero Santini was not just a great jumping rider, but a great rider in all disciplines, at a time when the line between disciplines was blurry, and in Santini's case, nonexistent. During his lifetime, Santini was considered the greatest riding teacher in North America, bringing his direct knowledge from Caprilli, the inventor of forward seat jumper riding.

The Forward Impulse describes in simple language how to balance the horse through engagement of the haunches, enlightened use of the seat, and conscientious elasticity of the rein contact. Not one in a hundred riders has access to the kind of teaching that focuses on the controlled energy of the haunches. Too many riders are satisfied with uninspired gaits offered passively by the horse. This book puts the focus where it belongs: first on the engine; then, on the system of aids that manages that power to create an opportunity for the horse to express himself with magnificent gaits.

Xenophon Press is proud to offer the opportunity for riders to see for themselves how logical and systematic this dream can be.

Frances A. Williams, M.D.
Editor, Xenophon Press

*It is far more difficult to be simple
than to be complicated.*

—JOHN RUSKIN

PREFACE

THE main subject of this, my second book on the Italian Method of Equitation, is the action of the hand and its relation to the natural forward balance of the horse—the *"impulso in avanti"* [forward impulse — *Editor's note.*] typical of the modern Italian School. I wish, however, also to call particular attention to two of its subsidiary chapters, namely those on polo and on the side-saddle; both subjects are, I think, worthy of dispassionate consideration from the angle of the thirty-five-year-old "new" theories which I have taken upon myself to explain to the English-speaking riding world.

With regard to polo, it is only reasonable to state that, it being a game new to Italy, whatever theories are now put forward in this country in relation to it must perforce be considered tentative. As, however, by the light of logic there is no reason to discard *a priori* the Italian ideas of seat, hands and horse's balance as inapplicable to a game in which so far rough-riding has been taken for granted and raised no protests, we should not exclude the possibility of "IL SISTEMA" [the system — *Editor's note.*] eventually coming into its own in this field, as in every other. For the Italian version of polo really to attract the attention of such as have preceded us on this particular road by many years, it may be necessary for Italians to make as characteristic and successful an appearance on the international polo stage as our horse-show team did at Olympia in 1908. This—provided that while we master the game thoroughly we also breed or import horses of the necessary quality and instruct them according to our own methods—may not be so remote a possibility as one might be led to suppose by the extreme youth of the game in Italy.

The most elementary principles of forward riding have been more mishandled and worse distorted in relation to the side-saddle than in the case of the cross-saddle, as I think anyone with an open mind will agree.

I know that it will be considered daring and perhaps unconvincing for a member of the male sex to deal with a subject only women of long practice should approach, but since no forward seat side-saddle creatrix [*a female creator — Editor's note.*] has yet appeared, I make bold to submit the suggestions of a mere man who can, in any case, add to his considerable practical and theoretical knowledge of riding in general, the deductions of not unsuccessful experiments.

—Piero Santini.
New York, June 1936.

ILLUSTRATIONS

Tor di Quinto—1906 (*Frontispiece*)

NUMBER
1   Fall probably due to pull on reins....................12
2   The Italian position in emergencies....................12
3   Horse taking off too close and sideways....................13
4   Horse's mistake remedied by forward hand....................13
5   Putting weight forward to avoid error....................18
6   Jumping smoothly....................18
7   Example of untrammelled extension....................20
8   Example of flexibility of foot....................20
9   Straight forelegs on landing....................25
10 One-two landing movement of forelegs....................25
11 Straight line from shoulder to mouth....................29
12 Straight line from elbow to mouth....................29
13 Preserving balance by hanging on the reins....................30
14 Separation of centres of gravity....................30
15 Resuming stride without effort....................32
16 Effort of resuming stride after landing....................32
17 Effort of resuming stride after landing....................35
18 Seated....................46
19 Left behind....................46
20 Right way to rein back....................53
21 Wrong way to rein back....................53
22 Relaxed halt....................54
23 American Steeplechase—The "Liverpool" at Brookline....................55
24 English Steeplechase—The "Open Ditch" at Liverpool....................55
25 "Lightening the Forehand.."....................56
26 American flat-racing seat....................57
27 English flat-racing seat....................57
28 The Italian seat in the hunting field 59
29 At a Roman meet....................59

v

30	American hunting seat.	61
31	Italian hunting seat.	61
32	Example of deliberate reliance on reins.	69
33	Example of deliberate reliance on reins.	69
34	A forerunner—Leslie Cheape.	75
35	Perfect swing from the hips.	79
36	Downward movement of horse's head in stopping.	80
37	The high hand and the low hand.	80
38	Good forward position in polo.	82
39	The high hand in polo.	83
40	The seated position in polo.	83
41	*Écrasé* [crushed] position inevitable with present side-saddle	90
42	Excellent example of left leg and foot in correct position.	90

ILLUSTRATION

DIAGRAM
A   Italian Position...5
B   Collection..8
C   Extension..9
D   Positions of Horse's Head...27
E   Arms and Hand Positions...36
F   Hand Positions...38
G   Side-saddle Positions...89

SKETCHES [by Paul Brown]
High School...16
The Nasty Place...34
Hopping on One Foot..49
"Open Jumping.."...61
A Study in Hand Positions..61
Disorder...93

I: THE FORWARD IMPULSE

A WELL-KNOWN novelist describes writing as "one long headache." If this definition applies to purely imaginative works in which meticulous accuracy of expression may be an added merit but is not of vital importance, to make one's meaning clear in words on the technicalities of any particular sport is a strain comparable only to the punishment of Sisyphus [the son of Aeolus, punished in Hades for his misdeeds in life by being condemned to the eternal task of rolling a large stone to the top of a hill, from which it always rolled down again. — *Editor's note*.]

For example, immediately on the appearance of a volume in which I flattered myself I had described with almost painful accuracy exactly what the forward seat consists in, someone wrote me that Fred Archer was its first exponent—information which might well have left me perplexed had not my correspondent been quite ingenuously explicit and added "because he rode with a long leather with his face parallel to the horse's neck, *which made it a forward seat."*

The names of well-known sportsmen who have in past days apparently practised the forward seat with good results have also been quoted.

I have never excluded the possibility that sporadic instances of individual styles resembling the present Italian system may at intervals have been adopted, and I would be the last to marvel at their success, but it is undeniable that forward riding as a complete method for both man and horse appeared for the first time thirty years ago in Italy and spread all over the world, thanks to the officers of some thirty nations listed in Appendix A of the present volume.

To avoid every possibility of further equivocation, let us understand each other once for all by momentarily taking the word "seat" in its anatomical sense.

Visualizing it therefore not as "that quality which permits the rider to remain master of his equilibrium whatever may be the actions of his horse," but as that part of the human body which comes in contact with the bottom of a chair, when, with the latter idea in mind, we say "forward seat" we shall deliberately want to signify a position in which the seat or buttocks are forward—that is, nearer the middle than the cantle of the saddle. As this definition, however, does not exclude a perpendicular position of the body, we must at least mentally add "and one in which the rider rises from the saddle leaning the torso forward proportionately to pace and effort." If the body is only bent or flattened forward the seat should not be called *the* or even *a* forward seat, no matter how forward hands and arms may be, not to mention, like my friend, the face!

I incline to think that if instead of writing a book on the forward seat—an expression by now worn threadbare and shabby by being dragged *à tort et à travers* [Editor's note: "without rhyme or reason"] through all the riding communities of the world—I had mainly dealt with less evident but just as important characteristics of the Italian school, I would have rendered my readers a better service by getting their minds into a fresher groove, and striking nearer to the core of the excusable ignorance of such as have really never been in possession of the elements indispensable to a complete grasp of the subject.

The most obvious feature of the Italian method is, of course, the position of the rider's body from the waist down, but there could be no greater error than to conclude thereby that the whole conception of Italian horsemanship here begins and ends, or that the Italian system in other respects resembles those which held the stage until early in the present century and to a great extent continue to do so. Its very foundations are not only different but antagonistic, and based on a theory of the horse's balance and the horseman's action of the hand both entirely new—thirty-odd years ago—in the history of equitation.

Certain very recent contemporary schools of horsemanship claim to have taken the best from every system, thereby tacitly inferring that they have composed perfect wholes.

So far as the Italian system is concerned any such admixture is an impossibility, and a hard-and-fast mechanical impossibility at that, for its various parts are as interlocked as the component pieces of a particular mechanism; the forward seat is dependent on what the Italian Cavalry Regulations term the "forward impulse," and vice versa; the position of the foot affects the knee, and a certain peculiar type of action of the hand is necessary for the preservation of the forward balance, and so on and so forth. The true forward method must therefore be accepted *in its entirety*, and not applied piecemeal, or grafted on to other systems, and the fact that these latter courses have almost invariably, unconsciously or deliberately, been followed, not only by civilians but in military schools as well, largely accounts for poor results and dire confusion.

We can convince ourselves of the indivisibility of the Italian principles of balance, seat and hands and all their component factors by, for example, taking a position at first correct in every detail (Diagram A) and then suddenly jerking the tibia from an oblique to a vertical position, bringing the foot at right angles to it: we will see at once that this is sufficient to shift the whole position and interfere with every principle of the method. The same can be demonstrated in different ways, by any other modification of the proper balance—by pointing the toe down instead of up and out, which loosens the knee, by straightening the leg, foot forward, etc., etc. We could go on indefinitely, but these examples are, I think, amply sufficient to illustrate the impossibility of taking individual parts of the method and amalgamating them with others from different sources. The application therefore of any separate Italian detail to, say, the typical French school or German methods or vice versa only results in the monstrosities we are abundantly treated to in the international show-ring.

The problems which have faced riding humanity are two: how to stay on a horse and how to control him. The first has received anxious attention through the ages; the latter caused fewer sleepless nights, affecting as it did the horse's and not the rider's comfort; force as practically the only means of mastery was therefore accepted until the forward idea and attitude of mind of the contemporary Italian school definitely dawned upon riding humanity. It is these, not the seat *per se*, that are the real bases of modern Italian horsemanship, as conceived by Federico Caprilli.

Diagram A

A-B, C-D—*Parallels between which the leg below the knee should always remain. (N.B.—Only when leg is used as an aid can the heel be permitted to go behind the line C-D.)*

E-F—*Perpendicular behind which the body should never swing.*

G-H, I-J—*Horizontals, always to be imagined as parallel to the horse's spine irrespective of the attitude, above or below which the hands should never go.*

Arrow 1— *Direction of foot inclination.*

Arrow 2— *Direction of ankle.*

Arrow 3— *Direction of knee.*

Arrow 4— *Direction of hip-joint.*

Arrow 5— *Direction of loins.*

Arrow 6— *Direction of shoulders.*

Arrows 7, 8, 9 } *Brake-lines: heel-loins-hand control-and-halting action.*

Arrows 7, 8 } *Heel-and-loin pressure for jumping, steep inclines, refusals, pecks, etc.*

Diagram A

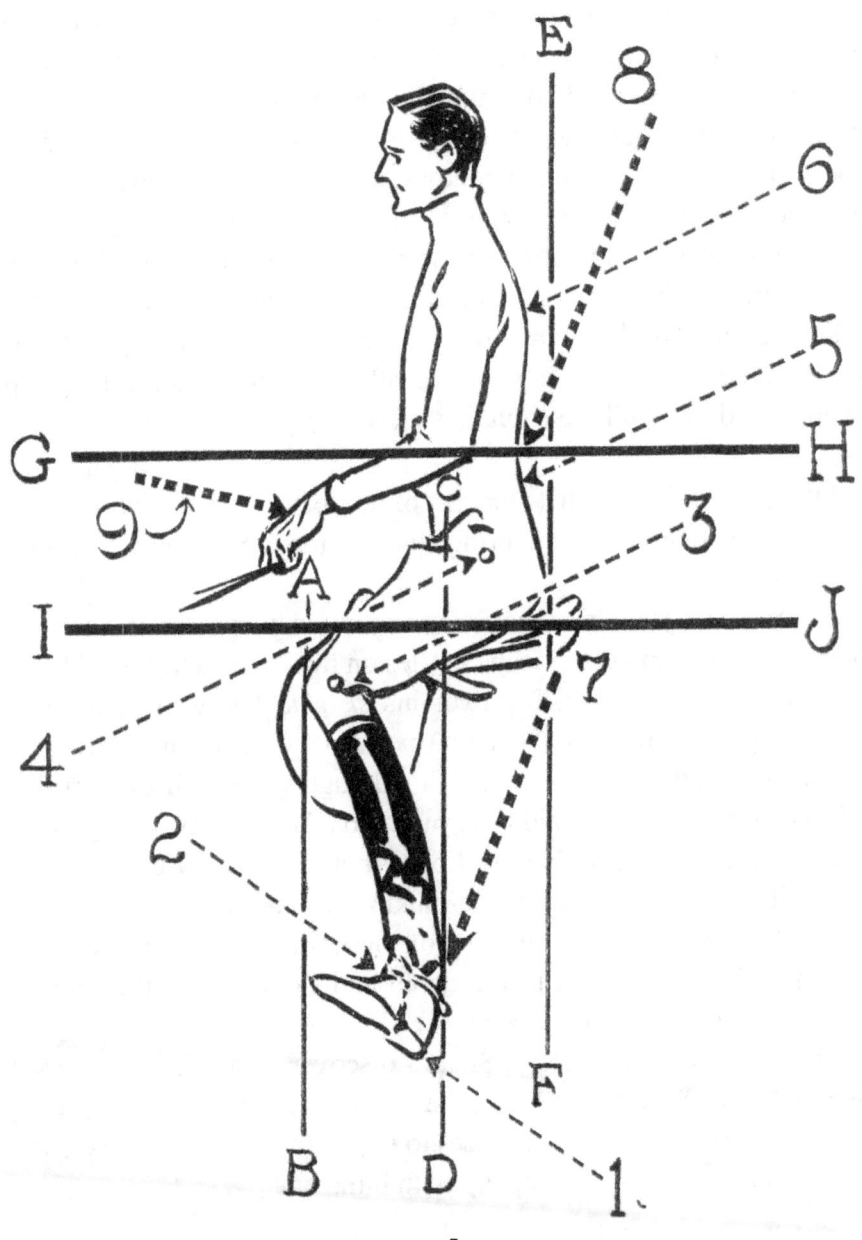

1897–1907

The last official impersonator of the old methods in Italy was Caprilli's immediate predecessor at the Cavalry School—Cesare Paderni, a horseman of undoubted worth, but the exponent of theories which had had their day.

Italian, but a civilian graduate of the Austrian Hofreitschule [Spanish Riding School], Paderni was imported to Pinerolo in the 'nineties to teach equitation to the young cavalrymen of United Italy. A few years later fresh ideas swamped both him and his partisans, and a simpler but more complete school made its entry into the equestrian world, mainly because, although a cross-country advocate in theory, in practice Paderni was handicapped by the "classicism" of his equestrian upbringing.

A synthesis by elimination of the sound principles of all time, the present Italian school was not the result of evolution—a word which implies continuity—but a *revolution*. Genius may be a capacity for taking infinite pains, but it is above all the ability rapidly to grasp essentials and as rapidly to exclude superfluities.

I think it but natural that students of the forward seat, Americans in particular, should never fail to bring up the name of Sloan in connection with its origin.

It is true that just about the time the American invader, in yachting clothes, was cracking champagne bottles on the devoted heads of Ascot waiters, Caprilli was puzzling over his *sistema* [system]. It is quite within the possibilities that the new American racing seat may have had an influence on the course of Caprilli's thoughts, it is self-evident that in the latter's straining to find a formula Sloan's idea may have given a beneficial fillip to Caprilli's reflections—but it is equally clear that, in spite of its far-reaching and epoch-making results, Sloan's was but an empirical and rudimentary solution of the immediate problems of the flat-racing field, compared to the depth and extension of the Caprilli method.

According to his own story, Sloan's discovery that a horse galloped faster with the rider's weight on the withers was the result of being obliged, as a small boy taking horses to water, to embrace the neck of a runaway so as not to part company with him.

Caprilli gave years of incessant toil to solving, in his exacting way, mechanical, physical and anatomical problems pertaining, not simply to galloping a racing distance on the flat, but to all equestrian possibilities and emergencies—jumping evidently not the least of them.

It took him, for example, practically all his riding life to determine whether the forward position should be applied to descents, especially at precipitous angles, a question he decided only a few months before his death in 1907. The frontispiece shows the slide at Tor di Quinto in the spring of that year, just before the Italian Cavalry School's definite break with the last vestige of the past.

Endowed with a sense of humour—even at times of a sardonic quality—he seldom failed to find amusement in his weightiest ponderings. His most original combination of duty and play was the fitting to the back of his favourite mare—his inseparable companion in experiments—of a straw-stuffed dummy of the kind used in all armies for sabre or bayonet practice. Left to her own devices in the Tor di Quinto stable-yard with this life-size puppet on her back, the mare entered whole-heartedly into the spirit of a game of tag with the captain's troopers, while Caprilli studied her movements in her efforts to escape the encircling soldiers, and the manikin's reactions thereto.

Sloan has left us his "Life," which enlightens us not at all regarding the only side of it which could have been of real interest—the whys and wherefores of his own particular style and the technical reasons of its success. We are therefore justified in concluding that he was incapable both of description and analysis and that all that could be expected of him was the almost unconscious contribution of one embryonic idea.

The very little that Caprilli wrote concerns not his person, but is a remarkably striking and clear exposition of conclusions which, at the time, seemed as revolutionary as Galileo's opinions in the days of the immovable earth.

As, like his countryman and spiritual ancestor, [Giovanni Battista] Pignatelli[1], Caprilli had an antipathy to writing only second to his dislike for walking, we owe most of the very few pages he ever wrote to an

---

1   Famous Neapolitan horseman who, with Cesare Fiaschi and Federico Grisone, formed the great triad of Italian Sixteenth Century "Cavallerizzi" to whom the Renaissance revival of Equitation as an art is due.

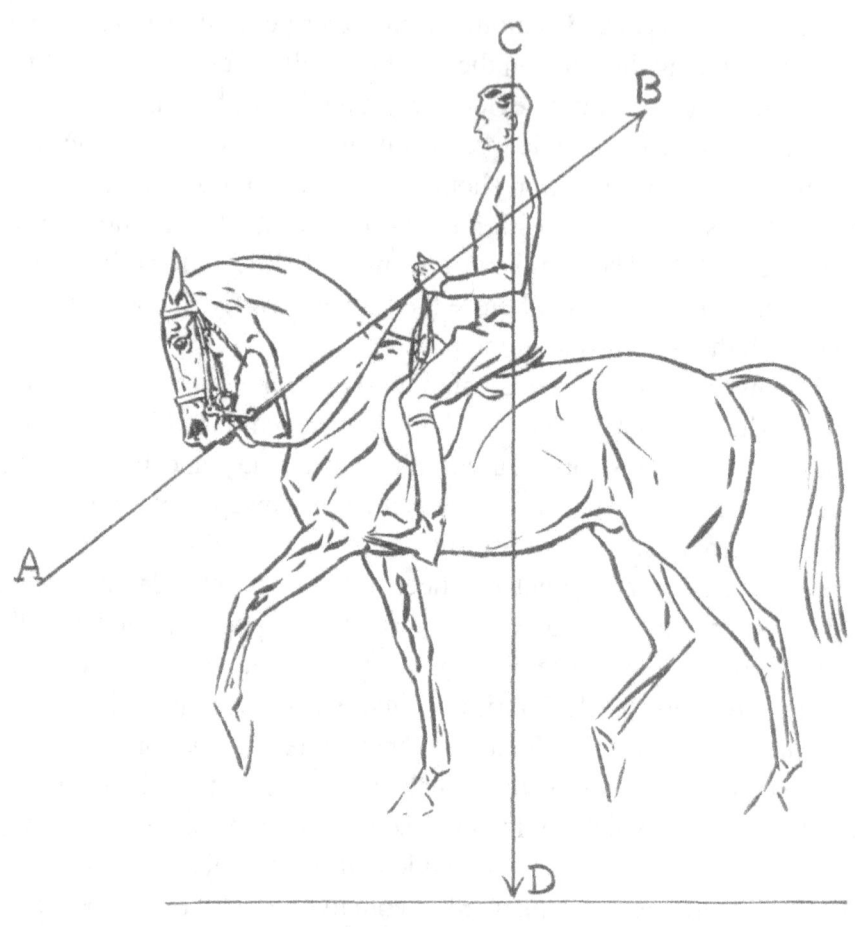

DIAGRAM B

*Collection. A-B—Backward and upward movement of hand.
C-D—Perpendicular of body weight.*

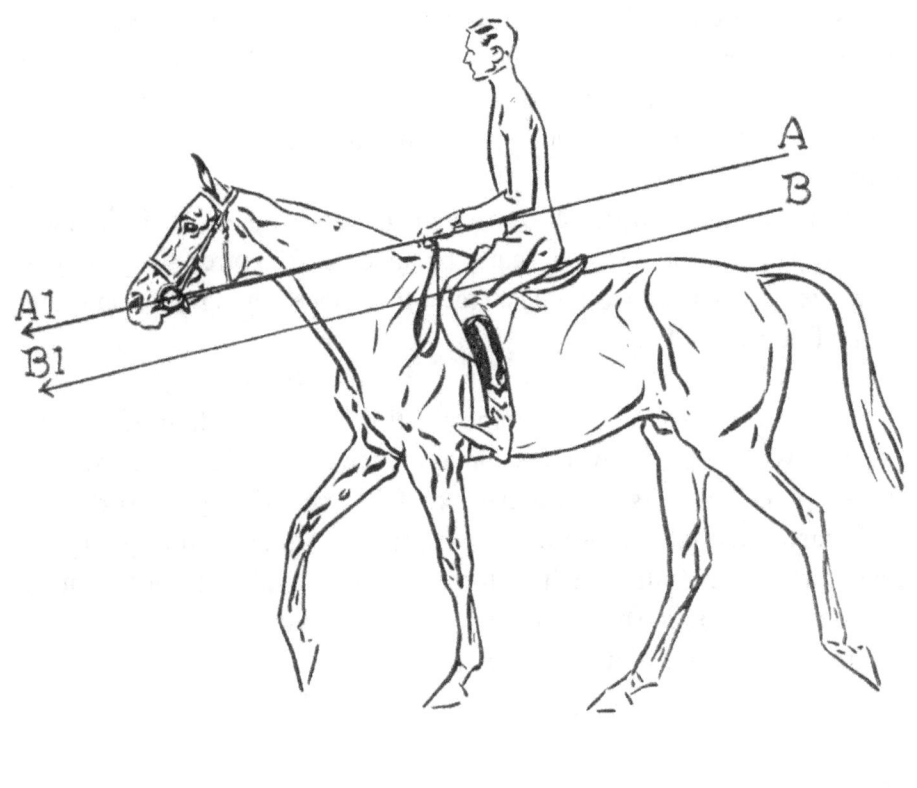

DIAGRAM C

*Extension. A-A¹—Forward movement of hand.
B-B¹—Direction of body weight and forward impulse.*

accident which kept him in bed for a fortnight. To while away the idle hours that crawled so heavily by, he dictated to his favourite pupil and devoted friend, Bianchetti, his undying "Principii." If some of the ideas contained therein strike us as truisms let us keep in mind that a great number of his tenets have by now been so generally accepted as part of our present attitude towards that willing but somewhat obtuse and impressionable child, the horse, that we have forgotten their original source.

Caprilli furthermore was an even greater student of the horse's psychology than he was of seats, balances and centres of gravity—which is his greatest and noblest claim to a place among the Immortals of the Equestrian Art.

To go into his method of domestication and instruction of the colt (there never was such a word as "breaking" in his vocabulary) is beyond the scope of the present volume and is in itself a subject worthy of undivided attention, so profoundly intuitive is its dissection of equine mentality, so smoothly do its educational phases fit into one another without a jar or a seam and, above all, without even the faintest semblance or suggestion of violence.

The Italian Method versus The High School

It is not necessary to enter into a detailed analysis of the methods of Caprilli's predecessors from the sixteenth to the end of the nineteenth century to perceive that their fundamental conception of the action of the hand and the consequent balance of the horse is identical and varies only in degree; the Hanoverian bit [Hanoverian Pelham bit has a large port, which applies tongue pressure, and rollers on the mouthpiece. — *Editor's note*], still in honour in some armies, continues to personify the original sin that has excluded horse and rider (the former particularly!) from the Equestrian Eden to which the snaffle is one of the keys.

The horseman of the past was a horse dominator and a horse breaker in the most aggressive sense of the word. Even now, in countries where the *haute école* still holds its baroque sway, the spirit is much the same; for example, the expression "attacking" a horse is current—this onslaught consisting in deliberately exciting defensive instincts merely for the sake of overcoming them with the aid of bit, whip and spur—and imposing accomplishments as useful to the instruction of a hunter or a charger as jumping through hoops would be to the shooting dog.

This constitutes the outward expression of the somewhat primitive idea that equitation consists in a struggle between man and horse in which the former must be the victor. If there is no spontaneous conflict the votaries of this school proceed to manufacture it, with what benefit to the horse's disposition we can easily imagine[2].

Even the mildest of Caprilli's predecessors went on the assumption that a horse should be *deliberately brought into his bridle and balanced by his rider,* with neck curved and head at right angles, at the very least, to the ground (Diagram B)—and from their point of view they were to a certain extent right because they started from an erroneous premise: they sustained that a horse in his natural state not being mounted, as soon as a weight is put on his back (the rider's in this particular case) his whole equilibrium must be changed.

To that the answer is that it all depends where and how we place the added weight. If we sit as in the days of Pignatelli their reasoning is irrefutable, but if, on the contrary, we place our weight in such a way as to conform to the horse's natural equilibrium (Diagram C), all necessity for establishing artificial balance vanishes into thin air.

It moreover should be the duty of the modern horseman not to interfere with his mount's natural action, but to sense favourable reactions in time to conform to them. The encouragement and preservation of the "forward impulse" constitute the very essence of a method in which all contractions and superfluous repressions are considered harmful and in contradiction to the principle that a horseman should strive to get from his mount *the maximum result with the minimum effort.*

---

2   "Any system of training that destroys the tranquillity of the horse is defective." U.S. Army Cavalry Training Regulations, 1922.

PLATE I.—*Fall probably due to pull on reins.*

PLATE 2.—*The Italian position in emergencies.*
The rider has kept his seat thanks to correct ankle and knee positions.

PLATE 3.—*Horse taking off too close and sideways saved by forward hand.*

PLATE 4.—*Horse's mistake remedied by forward hand (horse and rider on right).*

It is, therefore, a conception of equitation *entirely opposed* to the so-called "classic" school which can think of no better way to get a horse to place "all his active forces at the disposal of the rider" than by bringing his forehand and quarters together "like the two ends of a curved whip." This is called a "state of equilibrium, the stability of which may be broken at the slightest demand by all the forces of the horse which are tense and ready to act." How useless are such repressions for outdoor practical purposes is proved by the unguarded admission that this equilibrium requires such "muscular tension" that it should not be employed when the maximum speed of any gait is required, as it exacts a position of the neck and a suppleness of jaw and poll "unfavourable for speed." For any really practical purpose, who would strive to *reduce* a horse's speed?

Italy has long ago repudiated all *haute école* theories and abandoned all application of them as contrary to its own conception of out-of-door horsemanship. Really to ride therefore *all' italiana* it is indispensable that the horse be left his natural poise—a proceeding in complete contradiction to the French school or its predecessors of the Renaissance and following centuries, to the Spanische Hofreitschule [Spanish Riding School], and above all to the rigid German method, the main object of which seems to be to reduce the horse to a spiritless automaton—which may serve very well for the show-ring but presents grave dangers when applied to cross-country work.

If we compare the Italian Cavalry Manual even to that nearest to it in simplicity—the English—we shall find that the former excludes the long-reins, the flexions and the bending which are the very basis of the colt's instruction in the latter. Even longeing is only exceptionally resorted to, in cases, for instance, of particularly difficult and obstinate subjects, to correct acquired vices and to exercise horses which for some particular reason, such as a sore back, cannot be ridden.

"It must be kept in mind *that work on the longeing rein can never take the place of mounted instruction* (i.e. from the saddle) of which it can, however, be a useful accessory[3]." The Italian natural system, of the utmost plainness from the training of the remount up, goes on the assumption that with a mute beast, which has preserved its primitive

---

3   "Istruzione a Cavallo e Addestramento Ippico perl'Arma di Cavalleria," 1932.

construction and habits more than man, nature cannot be improved upon. Even the benefit a colt is supposed to derive from artificial gymnastics is attained better by natural outdoor work, just as from his first ungainly steps he gets his final balance and assurance with the unaided development of his muscles and of his senses by exercise, not *exercises,* in the open[4].

The Olympic Games

A critic of equestrian matters not very long ago informed his public that "there are but superficial points of difference between the ancient high-school which used the *piliers* [pillars] to develop the forehand *[sic],* or Baucherism which accomplished the same results from the saddle, and the scientific methods of Tor di Quinto"—this in spite of the fact that what has so far restricted Italian horsemen's part in the equestrian Olympic games is precisely the fundamental divergence between the Italian method and the "ancient high-school" or what was known in the past century as Baucherism.

It has been so far impossible for Italians to participate in anything but the jumping contests of the Olympic games because all else—notably the *dressage* competition—was based on principles radically at variance with those of our "natural" equitation. To such as have so far followed me this divergence will be evident, not as limited to a diversity of seat, but to the much deeper principle of the forward idea as against the general "backward" conception of horsemanship.

Just as, however, the Italian seat with time and experience has slowly but relentlessly gained ground the world over, so are other and still more radical Italian principles piercing the conservative armour of the official organizations in control of international equitation.

In November, 1933, the annual Congress of the International Federation of Equitation was held in Paris, and Germany, Austria,

---

[4] With the gradual development of his physique the colt acquires balance and cadence of his own accord quite naturally without any necessity for forcing him by uncalled-for action or special exercises. All of which results in his acquiring the right position of head and neck and the necessary flexibility of all parts of his body without the slightest necessity for obtaining them otherwise; normal progressive and rational work does the rest." Id. id.

High School.

Belgium, Bulgaria, Spain, the United States, France, Holland, Italy, Lettonia, Portugal, Poland, Sweden, Switzerland, Czechoslovakia and Yugoslavia sent delegates, while Denmark, Great Britain, Ireland, Norway, Romania and Turkey were present by proxy. All *dressage* tests of the Olympic games exacted the employment of means entirely alien and not admitted by our equitation, for it is necessary to employ in the execution of certain movements a balance substantially different from the horse's natural equilibrium, the respect of which constitutes, I repeat, *the basic principle which differentiates Italian equitation from all others.*

Italian requests that at least the conditions of the "Concours Complet d'Équitation" or three-day event be altered had always been refused, and the Italian Federation of Equestrian Sports had never been even permitted to be represented on the committee or among the judges—such schismatic heretics were we considered!

Finally, however, thanks in part to a practical demonstration of the Italian method given at Pinerolo in October, 1933, for the benefit of Commandant Hector, Secretary-General of the International Equestrian Federation (who reported so favourably on what he had seen that many of the Paris delegates expressed the desire to be similarly enlightened), the Italian suggestion that the three-day test be modified in accordance with our theories was allowed to be brought on the *tapis*. Ably and eloquently expounded by the Italian envoy, Lt.-Col. Piero Dodi[5], the logic of the arguments in favour of a revision overcame, in Paris, both the evident technical ignorance of some of those present and the open antagonism of others, and the necessity for modifying the conditions of the Olympic games equitation tests in accordance with Italian suggestions was finally admitted in the case of the three-day event.

With the invaluable support of General Detroyat, President of the International Equestrian Federation, the Italian envoy obtained the principal and most vital modifications asked for, namely:

1. *The suppression of the collected gaits,* and the resulting acceptance of the *forward balance,* which logically results in

2. The substitution of the expressions *"pas ralenti," "trot ralenti"* and *"galop ralenti,"* which imply only a diminution

---

5 President of the "Società Italiana del Cavallo da Sella," which forms part, with the Jockey Club and other executive bodies, of the Italian Federation of Equestrian Sports.

PLATE 5.—*Putting weight forward to avoid error.*

PLATE 6.—*Jumping smoothly.*

of speed (and no high action or change in the horse's *natural* balance), to *"pas rassemblé," "trot rassemblé"* and *"galop rassemblé" (rassemblé* meaning collected), which involve high action and balance on the quarters.

3. The suppression of all direct passing to the trot and gallop from the halt, in favour of progressive transition from the halt to the walk, from the latter to the trot and from the trot to the gallop.

What a conquest for the Italian method these modifications to the rules till now in force constitute, only such as have given the technique of equitation special attention can appreciate; the virtual recognition of the Italian natural balance on the part of other nationalities is infinitely more important than any success, no matter how spectacular, in either ring or field, for it constitutes, not the victory of individual horses or horsemen, but of an epoch-making axiom. The acceptance of theories in complete opposition to any so far admitted outside of Italy amounts to a capitulation of old methods before the invasion of the logic and practicality of fresh ideas, and the official ratification of the fact that Italian equitation is based on original principles of its own.

May this brief account of the latest development in the sphere of international equitation help to clear the fogs that so unaccountably and so irritatingly continue to shroud a method no longer in its infancy, and help the public in general and experts in particular to differentiate once for all between outdoor equitation and the inheritance of a "classicism" also originally Italian, but which has had its day. *(See Appendix B)*

Natural Attitudes

The difference between the two schools thus made clear, we can proceed to examine more closely why natural equitation requires a *natural* horse.

I have more than once had occasion to notice that those very countries in which bending, flexing, collecting and similar callisthenics are in honour are the very ones where most frequent recourse is had to strong bits and other contrivances intended to "hold" a horse, as a certain riding-master naively explained to me. A plain unaided

PLATE 7.—*Example of untrammelled extension.*

PLATE 8.—*Example of flexibility of foot.*

snaffle is hard indeed to discover in the very communities where such exercises form an inevitable part of the curriculum of tan-barked and resplendently mirrored riding "academies." This fact in itself constitutes a contradiction in terms, for if these gymnastics do render a horse so very handy, why is not a plain snaffle sufficient for one that has been industriously put through the whole gamut? In this connection another fact providing food for thought is that frequently a horse thus trained may acquit himself very well within long walls, but contrary to what is generally maintained, once in the open is not more amenable to the bit than his more natural brother—quite the contrary.

"Gathering," and the bits used in its application give this result, for it is but natural that a horse should attempt to avoid the pain inflicted on his mouth, just as he tries to reduce the discomfort of spur and whip "indications"[6] while twitching in the agonies of the passage, balotage, etc., etc. How much horses enjoy this sort of thing we can see by their eyes, ears and mouth; a horse happy in his work carries his ears pricked, keeps his mouth shut and has an entirely different expression of countenance.

It is extremely rare to find a horse that naturally refuses to meet his bit; like pullers, they are attempting to defend themselves as best they can from bad hands and bad handling.

The horse that, left to his own balance on a light bit, does not spontaneously take a slight hold is so exceptional as to be practically non-existent, for the natural attitude of a horse's head being roughly Line A-D of Diagram D it is only the wrong use of the bit and/or bending of neck and poll that causes the horse to put his head at a sharper angle unless deliberately made to do so by the rider's hand. As *we should never teach a horse anything that he can use against us,* let us remember that the action of the bit is as successfully annulled by contact of jaw to neck as by star-gazing and its consequent placing of the bit in the corners of the lips instead of on the bars. If a horse is behind his bit and attempts to escape its action, it is not so much due to bad training as to excessive schooling, often the result of too complicatedly "scientific" an attitude of mind on the part of the horseman who, if his mental

---

6   "Should the horse not respond to the action of the closed fingers the legs must act in such a manner as to force him on to the bit so strongly that it *causes him pain* and makes him seek to *escape it.*" (Author's italics.)
French Cavalry Regulations.

process has perchance taken the wrong turning, is likely to find himself one fine day weighed down by a mass of cumbersome and undigested knowledge which he is ever anxious to "try on the dog"—in this case his unfortunate horse.

The Horizontal Hand

The action of the hand as understood by the Italians constitutes quite as significant a departure from conventional theories as the seat itself, and is based on logic just as stringent, in complete contrast with the old principles, for of "natural" equitation it may be said *that the hands ever tend to advance, while in the old method they deliberately retreated;* in other words, the hands now follow the horse's mouth in all its natural movements, whereas they used to oppose and even practically suppress all instinctive action of head and neck.

To illustrate by a practical example what is meant by the complete avoidance of all unnecessary disturbing of the horse's balance and equanimity, let us take the most simple and elementary case of transition, i.e. from the halt to the walk.

I know from the practical experience of much observation that if you ask anyone to start his horse walking, ninety-nine times out of a hundred he will begin by what he considers the necessary "collecting" by briskly (when it isn't brusquely) raising his hands, giving the horse a jerk on the reins and a kick in the ribs—all of which, particularly the kick (the extreme *action* version of what should at most be an *indication),* is not only disturbing but generally quite uncalled for.

The Italian method, based on economy of the forces of both horse and man, admits of no squandering of energy. All transition, therefore, from one gait to the next is obtained with such a minimum of effort that the aids, if engaged at all, are of the subtle kind best described as invisible. If therefore—to return to our specific example—we wish our horse to break into a walk from the alert halt,[7] all we need to do is simply to advance the hand horizontally; the forward inclination of the

---

[7] N.B.— "Alertness" does not mean, or even imply, collection. The only difference between the relaxed and the alert halt is constituted by the complete absence of contact with the horse's mouth in the former case.

body will inevitably follow, the two being generally quite sufficient to signal our wishes to the horse's brain.

In cases of incomprehension or temperamental sluggishness, a slight momentary, not continuous, pressure of the leg—caused more by the stiffening of the calf muscles than by any actual visible accentuation of the tibia diagonal—can be applied. Anything more violent should be quite unnecessary, even in transitions to the faster paces, with a reasonably well-bred and not too lymphatic animal. The mere fact that we do—or rather should—shorten our reins progressively every time and just before we increase our gait and pace, synchronically accentuating the forward inclination of the torso, informs the horse naturally of what we expect of him. Incidentally, the ideal position of the hand in relation to the bit, to the horse's bars, and to his *balancier* is attained, *not only by its greater or lesser height with regard to the withers,* but by the preservation, at all paces and under all conditions, of the straight line formed by the forearm and reins from the rider's elbow to the horse's mouth—a straight line only slightly modified by the natural drop of the hand, by its own weight, from the wrist (Diagram E-A).

The above conception of the use of the hand has practically reduced its action to the backward and forward direction, all others being considered, under normal conditions, not only incorrect but detrimental. They belong to the histrionic or professional horse-show style of riding. As to disordered movements of arms and legs, in racing, especially in approaching jumps or riding finishes, very young gentlemen riders are the principal offenders, but if the sight of an enthusiastic amateur field nearing the winning-post is merely comic, that circular horizontal sand-sifting motion of the hands, vulgarly known as "washing clothes," sometimes results in tragedy when negotiating obstacles.

While considering the Italian conception of the action of the hand, let us examine a fallacy current in theory and in practice long before the days of forward riding.

I hardly ever open a book on equitation, even of such modern authors as should by this time know better, but I am informed that if a horse pecks on landing after a jump or risks coming down on his knees, he can actively be helped to right himself by the person on his back giving a pull—more or less severe or mysteriously subtle according to the individual temperament of the theorist—on the horse's mouth.

These instructions are, to be sure, qualified by grave reservations; we are told that only very experienced and very fine horsemen can successfully aid their mounts in this manner and that on the whole it is best for a novice (who thereby should feel duly humbled) not to attempt these higher flights of the equestrian fancy.

The truth is that not even the greatest horseman that ever lived could do any good in this way, for the advice so tendered is based on a physical error, or rather neglect or ignorance of a very evident physical fact—i.e. that we cannot prevent anything falling that we are falling with; if we could, aviation would become child's play. Contrary to helping a horse by a haul on the mouth as he is coming down on his nose, we thus inevitably insure his fall, for, if we jerk his head up we oblige him to drop his loins and quarters, and if we draw his head down—and therefore under him—we lend a hand to rolling him over. Judging by the perpendicular position of the horse, I feel that Plate 1 must be a good illustration of the latter result—and while referring to pictures in this connection a glance at another photograph (Plate 3) makes us wonder what would have happened had the rider been sitting down in the saddle or even giving the faintest pull on the reins instead of leaving his horse to work out his own salvation.

By none of which do I mean that the good horseman should always remain passive or even inactive.

In certain aspects of the initial phases of the jump, the rider with senses so highly attuned to his horse's that they become almost like a musician's ear, can put his weight more or less, and more or less rapidly—*but never brusquely*—forward on the ascending phase and at the vertex of the jump, according to what he feels his mount is asking of him and the manner and moment of asking. If, for example, a horse by mistake or owing to circumstances over which he has no control—such as crowding at a jump—takes off so close that he is obliged to practically rear to get his forehand safely over, his rider— hands more forward than ever—will have rapidly to put his weight very much higher forward than under ordinary circumstances (Plate 5), by straightening the legs the moment he senses the situation. In the opposite emergency,

PLATE 9.—*Straight forelegs on landing.*

PLATE 10.—*One-two landing movement of forelegs.*

that is, when a horse takes off too soon and consequently farther from the jump than normal, we should act as in the case of water-jumps and get as horizontally ahead of our horse as possible (Plate 7), hands again forward in the direction of the horse's mouth. Neither of these actions has anything to do with what is currently termed "giving the office," for we are not by them asking the horse to react to our bidding but only conforming to an initiative of his own. Giving the office is an indication frequently dangerous, because seldom timed to perfection, and if a horse has been patiently and quietly schooled, he will know much better when to take off than the man on his back.[8]

Just as harmful as the agitated hand is the rigid and immovable fist, an error of all such as practise forward riding without the mental picture of the forward impulse in their minds; its almost inseparable accomplice is the "bridge," that leather yoke made by the hands and six inches or so of rein which cheatingly relieves the knees from their duty of keeping their owner in place when jumping or going downhill. This makeshift pins the horse's head to such a position that on approaching the obstacle, unable to obtain the freedom he requires and asks for, he either takes off too soon out of irritation and the hope of getting free by violence or, failing this, too close to the jump, which, his head in the wrong position, he either clears by rearing, bucking or bouncing, instead of slipping over smoothly as he would were he allowed to extend himself (Plate 6). Bouncing, furthermore, causing as it does the horse to land on forelegs more perpendicular than normal (Plate 9) constitutes the worst kind of strain on the tendons, for the forefeet touching the ground practically together prevent the full development of that "one-two" action by which Nature has taught the horse to break the shock of contact with the ground (Plate 10). Bouncing, by the way, is frequently the result of poor schooling, such as bad longeing over jumps —longeing in any case being a very difficult art, not to be attempted by amateurs.

If the new school discouraged peculiarities such as the habit, at one time considered the acme of elegance, of raising the right arm in the air when half-way over a jump (calling a cab), it has on the other

[8]   "The horse himself is the unconscious judge of what had best be done; only experience and instruction can guide him in the choice of the action best suited to the surmounting of a given obstacle and the performance of the jump." M. Pennaroli— "Il salto nelle sue fasi e nella sua meccanica." *Cavallo Italiano*—August, 1924.

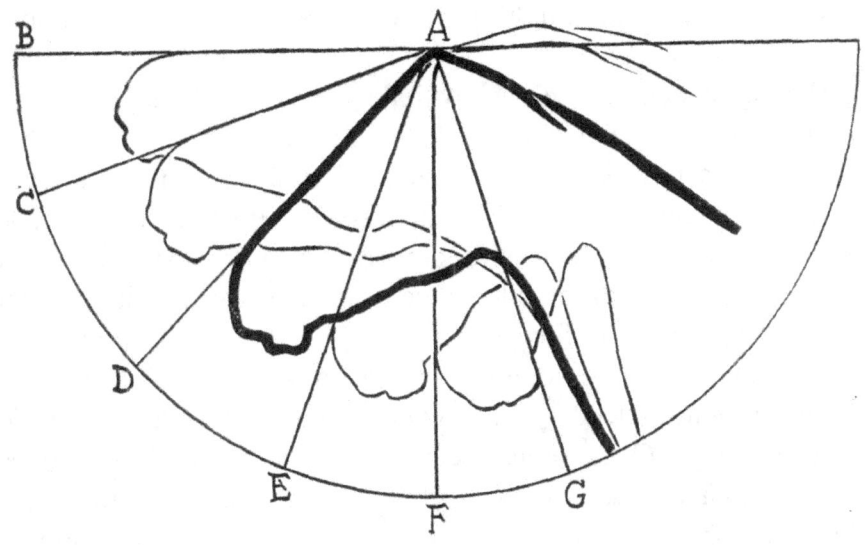

DIAGRAM D.
Positions of Horse's Head.

A-D—*Ideal (natural) position.*
A-E—*Intermediate position between the natural and the collected.*
A-F—*Perpendicular to the ground, typical of collection.*
A-G—*Extreme bent position.*
A-C—*Extension in maximum effort.*
A-B—*Star-gazing.*

N.B.—*A-G and A-B are positions of least control, the latter because nose is too high and the bit comes on the corners of the lips instead of the bars, the former because lower jaw is too close to the neck and the bars escape the action of the bit altogether.*

hand engendered what might be called vertical mannerisms almost as senseless.

Having renounced "milling" with the hands horizontally, vigorous horsemen seem to have to work off their abundant energies either by raising their hands high above the horse's withers or dropping them far below the line of the horse's crest; in some extreme cases the hands are first thrown into the air as the horse rises at a jump and then pushed well below the level of the rider's knee with a hearty pumping motion worthy of conscientious firemen.

It is apparently difficult for people to realize that violent exercises need not be done violently—on the contrary, that owing to their intrinsic vehemence it is all the more necessary to trim them of superfluous movement. Unnecessary throwing about of arms and legs corresponds in horsemanship to ranting on the stage, a characteristic of barnstorming Thespians, never of first-class actors.

I have already said that the movement of the hands should be limited to the horizontal and that the arm and forearm should never form either an acute angle or a straight line (Plate 11). It is, on the contrary, the elbow-to-mouth straight line already mentioned which should as much as possible be preserved in all circumstances (Plate 12). If we give this point the consideration it deserves we shall see that any other position disturbs the horse's mouth by causing confusing variations of contact and changes in the position of the bit—even if a plain snaffle—on the horse's bars, because perplexing shortening and lengthening of the reins result.

The straightest line between two points—in this particular case the horseman's elbow and the horse's mouth—being also the shortest, it naturally follows that if we raise or lower the hand and forearm this line is broken into an angle at the elbow, with the consequence that—unless we lengthen the reins by letting them slip through our fingers—the horse receives unintentional signals which mean nothing: they belong to the same category as digs with heel or spur caused by defective position of foot.

If, in Italy, the "heels down" refrain is incessantly drummed into us, a warning no less familiar concerns the hands, which are never allowed to take up their definite residence in any particular spot, such as, for

PLATE 11.—*Straight line from shoulder to mouth.*

PLATE 12.—*Straight line from elbow to mouth.*

PLATE 13.—*Preserving balance by hanging on the reins (the consequences can be appreciated by observing the horses and riders on extreme right).*

PLATE 14.—*Separation of centres of gravity.*

example, the withers. The hands, in other words, must be tranquil but not pinned anywhere; they should, on the contrary, continually follow the slightest movement of the horse's mouth, and at any pace above a walk be kept well apart from each other with reins entirely separate —laterally within the width of the horseman's body, and horizontally between the lines of the waist and of the knee (Diagram A).

Contact and Gravity

As I have had occasion to say before, the loose rein is not one of the maxims of the Italian method—far from it—but contact with the horse's mouth very decidedly is—contact of two different qualities, for which in Italian we have names as expressive as they are untranslatable.

In English the word includes all action of the hand on the horse's bars, and its shadings—even when the position of the horse's head alters its natural angle of, roughly, 45 degrees with respect to the ground—are only qualified by the adjectives "lesser" and "greater." In Italian, on the contrary, we have two separate words, one—*contatto* [contact]—implying that light touch which does not go beyond keeping the horse in a condition of attention, while *appoggio* [support] is used to describe the varying degrees of contact in relation to pace and control.

To use the horse's mouth as a sort of sheet-anchor for the preservation of one's balance and seat (Plates 13 and 14) is the most serious of all crimes against the forward impulse, and between it and the right degree of *appoggio* there is a very chasm, only bridged if we have developed through knee and ankle a seat entirely independent of the hand, and we keep our weight where it is most in accord with our mount's movements; it is because of this necessity that I dwell on a species of contact, the relation of which to the forward impulse is of fundamental importance to effortless performance for both man and horse. The horseman on the right of Plate 15 shows a case in point at the moment the horse resumes his stride after landing.

It stands to reason that if a rider is to be one with his horse —the only way to obtain smooth and synchronic action—he should strive not only to go with his horse but with the horse's centre of gravity. This lies, at the halt, at the intersection of a horizontal drawn at the height of the point of the shoulder and of a perpendicular dropped from the

PLATE 15.—*Resuming stride without effort, owing to rider's forward position.*

PLATE 16.—*Effort of resuming stride after landing, due to weight of rider on loins.*

withers. As in action, notably in galloping and jumping, the centre of gravity is shifted forward, the rider's weight must promptly conform to its modifications—a result only attainable in its perfection through the proper forward attitude of the hand which causes the weight of the man never to be left behind that of his mount. Incidentally, the application of this principle is of paramount importance in long jumps (water, brooks, ditches) at which the trajectory described being flatter than in high jumps (rails, walls, hurdles) and therefore resulting in greater initial abruptness, we are more likely to find ourselves seated (Plate 18) or left behind (Plate 19), unless, as the horse leaves the ground, we get so far forward as almost to precede his effort.

In pulling up—an accomplishment rarely given the attention it deserves—assuming that the hands have been consistently held forward on the right length of rein (as important above the waist as the right length of leather is below it) and contact has been thereby preserved, the correct way is to draw the elbows gradually back, preserving but gradually diminishing the forward inclination of the body from the hips; at the same time the heels are pressed down, the loins hollowed and the hand drawn back (Arrows 7, 8 and 9 of Diagram A). This leaves the position of the horse's head within the right limits, and his natural balance undisturbed, whereas if we pull up by thrusting our feet forward and raising the hands to the chest the first is fundamentally altered and the second destroyed. Backing should be executed by exactly the same means (Plate 20).

Expect that *appoggio* should decrease instead of increase, this is also the way to go down steep inclines, for it is obviously the only position in which they can be faced body forward with any success except by leaning hands on withers or neck—a practice incompatible with a school of riding that does not admit fixing the hand to any given point.[9]

Even if the forward position down steep inclines is not always perfect, it is at least gratifying to observe that horsemen the world over have at last realized the advisability of leaving the horse's quarters free in this emergency also; the forward position downhill was not adopted for the thrill it gives both performers and spectators, but because it was proved that the horse used his hind feet as a brake; hence the necessity

---

9   See my article "Riding Props and Bridges," *Polo Magazine*, April, 1935.

The Nasty Place.

PLATE 17.—*Effort of resuming stride after landing due to weight of rider on loins.*

for leaving the quarters to move without the rider's weight causing them either to be left behind or placed too far forward—both dangerous extremes. Needless to say, if it is advisable to keep a horse straight at his jumps, downhill it is absolutely indispensable, any sideways motion being inevitably bound to end in the disaster of a roll on the flank.

Reins

One of the main characteristics of the forward-impulse style of riding being elasticity, the way of holding the reins advocated in the past and still in all-too-general use is inadequate, for the actual position of the hand, and to an equal extent the way the reins are adjusted in it, have an infinitely greater influence on the horse's mouth than most of us imagine.

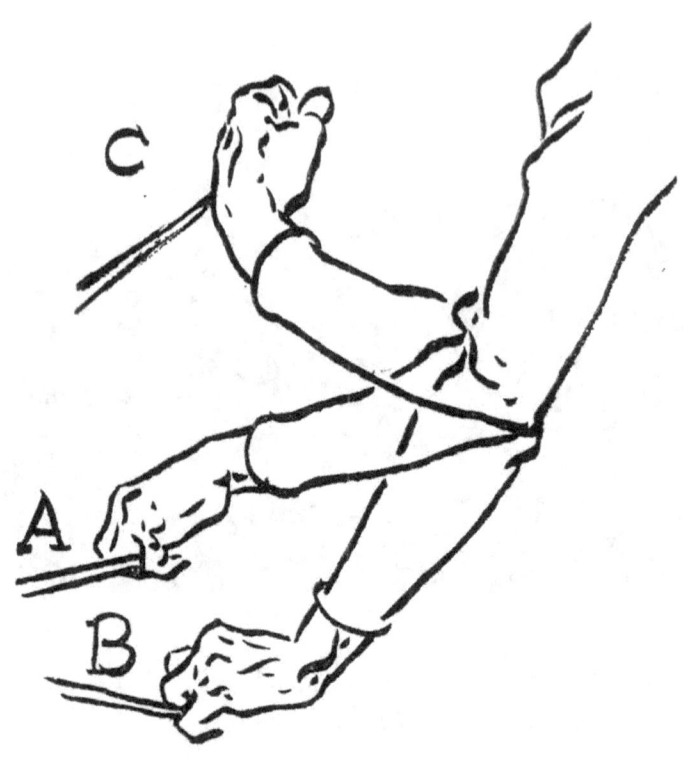

DIAGRAM E
Arms and Hand Positions.

A—*Ideal position of hand and arm.*
B—*Straight arm—hand too low, wrist dropped lower than knuckles.*
C—*Arm too bent, hand too high.*

Although the easiest, most logical and most practical way to hold two reins is what is called the "Nelson wrap," and with four reins a similar method which allows division of right and left between the two hands, the greatest advantage this arrangement offers is to allow us to drop our hands naturally, as if playing the piano, or as they would fall by their own weight were we to lay our forearms up to the wrist on the arms of a chair (instead of stiffly, thumb up, as shown in Diagram B), the superfluous length of rein falling between them, straight down and along the horse's right shoulder. The raised wrists and the horizontal knuckles, allowing complete relaxation, cannot but result in greater lightness of touch and in the greatest possible ease of movement, especially when the hand is required to advance as in 1, 2 and 3 of Diagram F. The lack of resiliency resulting from the old thumbs-up "collection" theory translates itself in harshness on the horse's bars.

Another detail of not negligible importance, as the reader can easily prove to himself by very simple practical experiment, is the placing of the rein when using the plain snaffle. That in all the diagrams which deal with the reins and in all the photographs of Italian horsemen contained in this book the rein is held between the fourth and little finger is not a matter of chance but of deliberate system. With the single-rein snaffle method—which is ours in all its simplicity—it will be found that, as less effort and therefore less stiffening of the fingers is required if we have the rein on the inside of the little finger, this position will make our touch lighter and control just as powerful, if not more so.

It is well to keep in mind that when it becomes necessary to bring a certain degree of force to bear, action should not be so much a matter of fingers and wrist as of pectoral and shoulder muscles, for the farther from the bars and bit the actual stiffening begins the less hard will it be. Except therefore in extreme cases when we wish, or are obliged deliberately to bring severe action to bear, the hold on a horse's mouth should begin not from the hand, but much higher up, the stiffening gradually creeping down to the fingers if necessary. In nine cases out of ten, however, rigidity will not need to reach the wrists before the horse will have responded.

The positions of the wrist shown in Diagram F–1, 2, 3 are part and parcel of forward riding which definitely excludes the stiff or immovable

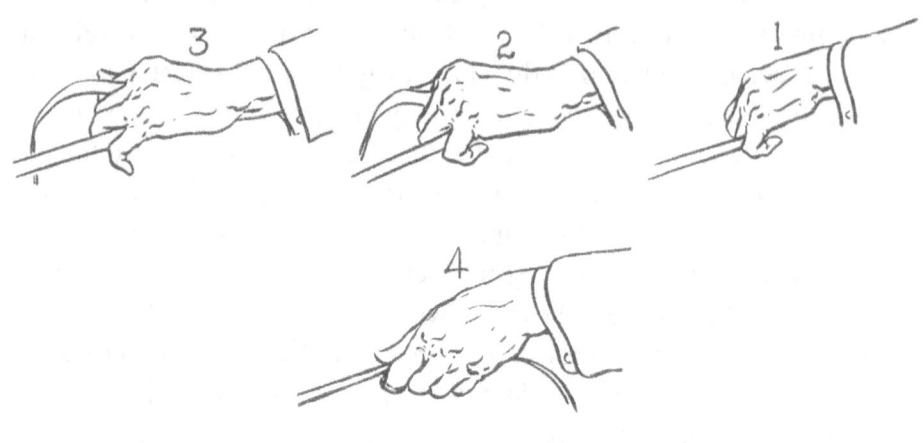

DIAGRAM F
The Hand.

1-2-3—*Its three consecutive advancing—
and, inversely, retreating—positions.*

4—*Present show-ring way of holding reins.*

hand even when inactive. Under ordinary circumstances the play the wrist is allowed by Position 1 is sufficient to permit that freedom of mouth far from incompatible with contact, which instead increases to an unnecessary degree—unless we leave the reins loose—the moment we turn our thumbs up and stiffen the wrist. It is practically impossible to develop any subtle action, particularly of the snaffle or bridoon, in this position of the hand—a fact which perhaps partly explains the poor results obtained with the plain snaffle in certain quarters and its consequent unpopularity!

For the majority of other ways of holding the reins there is no particular reason beyond the fashions and affectations of the passing moment of which the show-ring is the principal nursery. The sounder a horseman's knowledge and the more extensive his experience the quicker will he wave them aside, as he will wave aside the variety of gadgets invented, also generally for show-ring purposes, in the last few years.

For instance, the system shown in Diagram F-4—buried without honour in Italy, after a remarkably brief existence, in the year of grace 1917—is now having its day elsewhere. It is supposed to lighten the action of the hand. It so resembles a driving position that a show-ring rider applied it a year or so ago with the further improvement of loops in which to slip his hands, exactly as if he were driving a trotter instead of riding a jumper; this may be effective with a puller in the ring, although it is hardly necessary to point out its defects and dangers if applied to the open. Inversely, without the loops, I challenge anyone thus to control a horse effectively the moment any sort of trouble begins. I have more than once seen hasty and undignified relapses to a more logical hold in cases, for example, of run-out or refusal.

II: THE STIRRUP
Mounting and Dismounting—with and without

NOT one person in a hundred knows how to mount properly, and as to dismounting the least said the better. Although one of the recognized uses of the stirrup—besides that of giving the rider a *point d'appui* [fulcrum: the point on which a lever rests or is supported and on which it pivots. — *Editor's note*.] other than the horse's mouth—is to help the horseman reach the saddle, it is better, when young, to vault like the Italian trooper, and if "aged" to get "a leg up" whenever possible.

However quickly or lightly we may manage to mount, unless someone holds the off leather, weight on one iron inevitably causes the saddle to shift, even if ever so slightly; the results are often sores caused by twisted hairs. Were I therefore making a list of riding "don'ts" I would certainly include getting on a horse by the stirrup except when absolutely necessary, even though my countrymen have occasionally been criticized, and even ridiculed, in communities where assistance, except for jockeys, and ladies riding side-saddle, is considered an affectation.

Nothing is more irritating to anyone who has at heart the comfort and well-being of the horse than to see people get into the saddle with a bump instead of sliding gradually into position. Although neither the use of the stirrup nor vaulting excludes the latter system, the leg-up lends itself best to the avoidance of suddenly landing on the horse's kidneys with one's full weight; we should begin the sinking movement immediately preceding complete contact with the saddle by propping on a stiff right arm, and then on our knees. For the horse's greater comfort we can even go farther by remaining off the saddle by means of our irons and knees, until he has got into motion, an excellent precaution with nervous or over-sensitive animals.

Whether we do this or use the stirrup, in lowering our weight the right knee should be brought into contact with the upper part of the saddle flap as soon as it has passed the saddle's waist; it should then be slid gradually forward and down into its ultimate place, this last process to be accomplished very slowly, whereas the preceding phase—from the instant the right foot leaves the ground until it has passed the line of the horse's backbone—should be as brisk as possible, this to avoid both shifting the saddle and touching the horse with the toe.

These careful measures in mounting are not negligible details. As unfortunately even the best of us cannot always avoid upsetting our mount's equanimity, which we may have to put to considerable strain in the course of a hunt, a race or a jumping competition (particularly the last named!), we should make every effort to spare infliction of discomfort with consequent ruffling of temper; if we begin by getting on bickering terms with our horse, the chances are the rub will increase on the slightest provocation, whereas if we can contrive to stave off as long as possible all occasion of discussion we may even get to the end of the most imaginative show-ring course without having got on each other's nerves.

As mounting with the stirrup is of course frequently inevitable, it must be given its share of consideration.

Although, when mounting by the aid of the leg-up, the line of our shoulders should be parallel to the horse's spine, in mounting with the stirrup it should on the contrary be at right angles to it, with our back to the horse's head. In this position the effort of springing from our right foot and pulling ourselves up by the left hand on the pommel will be greatly aided by the horse moving forward as he generally does, especially when surrounded by others of his kind. Moreover, if the near rein or reins are kept a little tauter than the off, the semi-circular movement of the horse around the rider which will result will help swing the latter into the saddle; if, as explained above, we then slide our right knee against the off saddle flap as we slowly descend into place, we shall have accomplished the perfect mount, instead of, as frequently happens, hopping after him on one leg until, with a scramble, we land in the middle of his back like a sack of corn on a pack-mule.

Dismounting is every whit as important, and much the same rules apply.

Except for the very old, corpulent or rheumatic the aid of the stirrup to reach the ground should be unnecessary, and for the same reasons avoided.

If vaulting on to a horse's back, which should be done with the left hand half-way up the horse's neck and the other on the saddle pommel, presents difficulties to most people no longer in the first bloom of youth, vaulting off is infinitely simpler, for the law of gravity helps. What must, however, be eschewed is untidily and slowly sliding off with our waistcoat buttons scratching the saddle and our coat collar working up to our ears. As in everything connected with horsemanship trimness should be the word, we should first decide whether we really want to vault off or rely on the iron, and definitely do either one or the other, not a mixture of both.

Another and to me excellent way of leaving the saddle is by swinging the right leg over and sliding off, but in accomplishing this movement, in which it is best momentarily to drop the reins until the right thigh has passed the withers, two things must be kept strictly in mind:

1st—That *both* feet must be out of the irons before we initiate the first tempo, i.e. that in which the leg is swung over, for otherwise we risk the worst kind of fall on our face;

2nd—That as soon as we initiate the sliding-down phase we must twist from the hips in such a way as to land—on our toes and on bent knees—with our face to the horse's head and not with our back to his ribs. This also ensures our not losing our balance on landing, and automatically places us in the "stand to horse" position. This perfectly safe, quick and pleasant way of dismounting can become most dangerous if improperly or untidily executed; more than once in my experience have I had to "bawl out" people for bringing their right leg over before taking the left foot out of the iron—which induces me to consider the present warning neither pedantic nor superfluous.

The Foot and the Stirrup

Also of an importance much superior to that of a mere detail is the position of the foot in relation to the stirrup.

What is the reason for the Italian recommendation that the foot be well home in the iron—a recommendation most people seem to find so irksome to accept that they attempt on every ground they can think of to argue against it?

The main defect of a certain version of forward riding is a lack of finish, or rather of smoothness and of evenness of execution due to individual mannerisms—among them the tendency to keep the tread of the stirrup under the ball of the foot instead of putting the foot home.

It is perfectly true that the former position gives greater elasticity of ankle—in the purely vertical direction, however— but the reasons against it and against the drawbacks which ensue are sufficiently grave and numerous to counterbalance this one and only advantage.

To begin with the most obvious flaw, it is clearly easier to lose a stirrup thus placed than one which rests on the arch of the foot. Secondly—and this is more important—it is not possible to turn the sole out if the tread of the iron is across the broadest part of it, for the juxtaposition of these two flat surfaces prevents the ankle being twisted inwards so as to bring the sole out and the knee in and against the saddle.

The iron resting on the ball of the foot inevitably causes two displacements:

1st—If with the iron in this position we turn the foot out even ever so slightly, whether we turn the anklebone inward or not the knee is bound to detach itself from its proper habitat, leaving the famous triangle of light—which should never be tolerated—showing between knee and saddle;

2nd—Automatic contact between the two thus abolished, we are inevitably obliged to fall back on the lower part of the leg to keep us more or less in place—whereby we shall be reduced to doing with the tendon of Achilles what we should be accomplishing with the flattest part of the knee, to the utter destruction of solidity in the saddle. This is not only ugly but gravely defective horsemanship because:

(a) a loose seat causes disconnected performances disturbing to the horse;

(b) if our foot is not home in the stirrup it is easier to be pushed back towards the cantle or "left behind," and

(c) (last but not least) it makes it impossible for the whole part of the leg from the knee down to accomplish its proper function, for if we rely on the calf to keep our seat we sacrifice any action of the leg as an aid which, in the Italian method, is as important and effective, though simpler, than in any other.

Foot, Boot and Iron

In connection with the stirrup and its position in relation to the sole of the boot, I hope I shall be forgiven by all boot makers, famous or obscure, whose pride it is to turn out solid footwear, if I allow myself to express a few opinions in regard to the practicality—for the school of riding we are considering—of both the weight and shape of their productions.

By the light of what I have so far been at pains to explain I think it is clear that neither horse nor man should be deprived of any element of elasticity Nature may have endowed him with. Now, very heavy soles and their peculiarly curve-less waists, tend to stiffen both ankle and foot, for the straight waist obviously makes impossible that position of the foot in the iron we have just recommended, and thickness is of its very nature the opposite of resiliency.

For these reasons I have ever favoured a not-too-heavy sole, even when the dictates of fashion imposed the contrary. I am quite aware that in some countries—England, for instance—the heavier the hunting boot the better, climatically speaking; even there I have always been ready to sacrifice a little of my personal comfort, or make up for lack of impermeability of sole by the addition of an extra pair of socks, rather than renounce the feel of the stirrup tread so dear to the Italian cavalryman.

The Germans call a glove a hand-shoe *(Handschuh)*. Let us reverse this somewhat prosaic mental picture of what was once the noblest part of man's apparel, the symbol of chivalrous challenges and the proud perch of falcons, by momentarily conceiving the boot not merely as a highly polished but somewhat wooden object of apparel, but as a foot-glove, and as such attempt to visualize the function of what is in it contained. If we consider that the many small bones of which the foot is composed and the tendons

PLATE 18.—*Seated.*

PLATE 19.—*Left behind.*

and muscles which work them—quite as fine and sensitive and ingeniously arranged as those of the hand—have a right to their share in riding mechanics, we shall easily perceive why its sensibility should be as little diminished as is compatible with reasonable defence against the elements. No part of a horseman should be numbed and insulated, and although I shall not go so far as to say that we should ride, like the jockeys in the Far East, with bare feet and the outer stem of the stirrup between the toes, I sustain that a certain reasonable sensitiveness of foot contributes to good horsemanship. That the foot should and does give to the reaction of the horse, especially in the faster paces and in jumping, needs no proving. I give an example in Plate 8 in which the flexion of the foot in the stirrup, contributing to the general elasticity, is in evidence as a not unimportant factor in a strikingly good performance.

Stirrups, like bits, should be of burnished steel—never plated—large and heavy, and bell-shaped, not round, height from leather-slot to tread as much as six inches. When there is no particular reason for employing light stirrups weight is an asset, for a large heavy iron is more easily got rid of in case of emergencies and does not continue to follow the foot at moments when we prefer its room to its company.

Even as I say that stirrups should never be of the plated variety I realize how difficult it is not to use the various types of "never-rusts" at present on the market, for they save grooms the employment of burnishers—and elbow-grease— but I cannot refrain from calling attention to two points, one practical, the other purely aesthetic.

In the days when the new amalgams were unknown a broken stirrup or bit was practically unheard of; the rare cases I recall were due to very sharp and hard blows from falls or other accidental causes. Now, on the contrary, I see numberless irons and bits broken, and particularly twisted out of shape, in ordinary use.

As to the aesthetic reason for employing, if possible, the old type of bit and iron, there is as much difference between the appearance of burnished steel and of never-rust alloy (from the really smart workmanlike point of view) as between a pair of well-boned riding boots and patent leather *Chantillys;* the latter may shine more, but it is the wrong kind of glitter. Similarly, if we place the pure steel close to the composite we shall see at once how yellow is the latter and how tawdry.

Stirrup Accidents

Regarding the danger of being dragged by the stirrup, probably because of the size and shape of our irons, this sort of accident is so rare with us as to be almost non-existent. I personally do not recall a single one. The safety bars generally found on men's saddles are in any case either too easily opened, so that they are apt to leave us stirrup-less when we least expect it, or so hard and caked with dried saddle soap and dust as to never open under any circumstances; the consequence is that saddles are now being made in Italy with no safety appliances whatsoever and a steel ring is beginning to be used regardless of danger—because we do not believe the danger exists. As to the ladies, safety stirrups are of course never used by true *amazones* anywhere, and in Italy they, like the men, rely mainly on the size and weight of their iron to free the foot in case of falls—although the usual safety devices are of course to be found on all side-saddles, the large majority of which are still of English make.

Nothing should ever be added to the natural bareness of the tread of the stirrup itself; I mention this because I have more than once had occasion to detach and throw into the nearest gutter leather or even rubber appliances supposed to make the foot in the stirrup more comfortable. Those who cannot keep their foot right by natural means or cannot stand the sensation of the bare steel on the soles of their boots had better give up riding and take to some gentler pastime—croquet, for instance. Like a great many remarks of mine, the raising of this point may seem superfluous in a book obviously meant for horsemen of mature experience, but as I have seen these rubber and leather devices used in riding academies and clubs of a certain repute, my remarking on them is less idle than might at first glance appear. Incidentally, parents would do well to take note that if a rubber tread is applied to a child's stirrup, especially of the very small type, the chances of the child being dragged are increased a hundredfold—as they also are when children are allowed to ride in rubber-soled shoes.

Hopping on One Foot.

III: CROSS-COUNTRY ON ITALIAN PRINCIPLES
Misconceptions and Definitions

BOTH in England and America the Italian seat is still looked at askance for anything but show-ring purposes, the English sustaining that it is insecure, the Americans that it is cramped and uncomfortable. If the former—purely, however, from the angle of their traditional long-leathered "sugar-tongs" seat—may have at least the semblance of a case, the same cannot absolutely be said of the latter. It is difficult to conceive postures more cramped and/or precarious than those universally adopted, especially by the young idea, in the hunting fields of America; in this connection it may be interesting to mention that in the course of a couple of years of riding instruction in the United States I have probably lengthened more leathers than I have shortened to bring the knees of my pupils anywhere near their proper level. I found many thighs practically horizontal!

The epoch-making victory of our military team at Olympia in 1908 is, I fear, initially responsible for the legend that Italians are show-ring riders and nothing else, our method even in its worst imitations having, furthermore, ever since given consistently good results in this particular branch of horsemanship; to make matters worse, very few representative Italians have ever appeared in English or American hunting fields and none on English or American steeplechase courses.[10] The ill-considered conclusion has thereby been reached that our seat is all very well for plain sailing, but useless in any sort of heavy weather such as drops, pecks, pitching, refusals, bucks, kicks, etc. The "if the horse pecks" argument especially is considered irrefutable—a sort of knock-out blow to *all* forward seat theories—forward riding over the enormous drops and almost perpendicular slides of Tor di Quinto, which every foreign visitor to Rome can witness in the spring, being apparently ascribed to black magic.

At this point I must once for all and very clearly differentiate between "forward seat" and "Italian seat."

That the extraordinary postures taken by the civilian element in most countries outside of Italy are in no way applicable to cross-country riding of any description I am the first to admit, but as neither the Italian method—which is what we are dealing with—nor Italian military instructors are answerable for them, let us relegate them to the limbo of generic forward seats without accusing the Italian school.

The most apparent characteristic of our seat, superficially observed, not being so much the position as the shortened leathers, the average beginner, unless early enlightened, concentrates on this detail almost to the exclusion of all others, without even attempting to measure its influence on the general mechanics of riding which, if not treated with due thought and consideration, revenge themselves by inflicting that discomfort and constraint to which the misled foreigner takes exception.

The too-short leather then is the initial error responsible for the judgment so lightly passed on the Italian seat in English-speaking countries, although in reality it is more secure than any other mainly because of the downward-forward balance shown in Diagram C, aided by the pressure of the knee caused by the peculiar ankle twist by now familiar to such as have done me the honour of reading my first book.

---

10   An Italian who has done well in the professional field abroad is Riccardo Spano, who, in two consecutive years (1933 and 1934) has won, on a horse called Remus, the Grosser Pardubitz Steeplechase, run in October at Pardubitz, Czechoslovakia. Instituted many years ago by Count Kinsky, of Grand National fame, this race is run over a course of the same length as Aintree and, although most of the obstacles are of a different type, being generally wide rather than high, the race is admittedly one of the severest in the world.

PLATE 20.—*Right way to rein back.*

PLATE 21.—*Wrong way to rein back.*

PLATE 22.—*Relaxed halt.*

Even as an arch is made ever more solid the mightier the pressure put upon its keystone, the knees sink deeper into the saddle the greater the weight put on the irons. In a drop or a peck, therefore, the weight of the rider is riveted to his saddle, or rather saddle flaps—provided his ankles are flexed and his back hollowed—in directly increasing ratio to the brusque-ness of the jar and/or the steepness of the angle of the horse's descent towards the ground. It should here be mentioned that the relation between heel and loins is so very close that their downward pressure in the direction shown by arrows 7 and 8 in Diagram A should synchronize. We are pitched forward only if the back is rounded, the toes drop, and the feet swing back; these are elementary mechanics which apply in their entirety to the case of refusals as well, with the difference that if in the drop the pressure of the knee is increased in proportion to the sharpness of the angle of the drop itself, in refusals the reaction of the rider is limited to the horizontal level, aggravated by the brusque sideways twist of the horse's spine (Plate 2). Arrows 7, 8 and 9 of Diagram A might well be described as "brake lines," for such is really their action in all unexpected and unsettling emergencies, both on the

PLATE 23.—*American Steeplechase The "Liverpool" at Brookline*

PLATE 24.—*English Steeplechase The "open ditch" at Liverpool*

PLATE 25.—"*Lightening the Forehand.*"
Note foreleg bent back at the knee by impact of rider's weight on irons.

horizontal plane (refusals and run-outs) and the diagonal plane (the landing phase of the jump and the descent of inclines).

A foreign friend, by no means a novice in the equestrian art, expressed surprise at a steeplechase meeting in Rome, on seeing an unruly horse at the post lash out to the very sky a dozen times in succession without so much as disturbing by an inch the rider's very perched position in the saddle. Yet the explanation, applicable to bucking as well, is of an infantile simplicity; if we are not seated the reaction of the kick or buck is annulled because it does not reach its object; in other words, the horse moves between our knees and the violent reactions of his backbone expend themselves harmlessly on the empty air, without so much as touching the only part of the rider by hitting which he might unhorse him.

Kindred to the pecking objection is the argument against riding forward over blind fences because we cannot tell what is on the other side. To such as hold this view the only jump to be successfully negotiated

PLATE 26.—*American flat-racing seat.*

PLATE 27.—*English flat-racing seat.*

without sitting down and leaning back must be timber because it does not conceal the landing—but what we are supposed to do in any case once we are in the air and discover, say, a brook on the far side of a wall or a bullfinch, no one has to my knowledge ever attempted to explain.

Were we to confess that we are sometimes the victims of that very natural state of apprehension the stoutest heart cannot always control, and sit back at a fence in spite of ourselves to stave off till the last possible fraction of a second the impending realization of the superlative nastiness of a nasty place, we would, I think, be describing what really happens and the reason thereof. Incidentally, the habit of getting and staying forward can best be inculcated by reiterated practice in jumping on and off small banks, just as in the early training of a boxer the ability to counter is acquired by developing the impulse to meet what our instinct prompts us, on the contrary, to draw away from.

As I have before had occasion to explain at length, good riding, particularly of the forward variety, cannot be practised instinctively until all innate proclivities are reversed, and the reversal, not the original impulse, responds to the prompting of the brain. It being therefore instinctive to recoil from real or imaginary danger—which is the reason men who do the contrary sometimes get V.C.s—it is necessary uncompromisingly to suppress the original sin of the backward tendency when circumstances may be pressing us to think more of the cropper in the offing than the technique of modern riding!

If a horse has been sent too slow at a jump both high and wide, if he is tired, or his mechanical construction inadequate, whatever surprises the landing side may reserve, neither sitting back nor sitting forward will save us from the spill Fate has in store for us; indeed, in emergencies of this nature, of the two styles I choose the latter, for its worst enemy cannot deny it at least the merit of leaving the horse's loin muscles and backbone free to scramble and worm himself out of difficulties in his own way. Furthermore, contrary to all die-hard "backward" theories, it is in these cases much more unlikely for the rider to be prematurely thrown for reasons already explained, the sit-back position, on the other hand—especially if practised on the illogically short leather and straight forward leg of the present English steeplechasing school of thought—promptly catapulting him beyond the horse's ears.

PLATE 28.—*The Italian seat in the hunting field. Note forward inclination of body even at halt.*

PLATE 29.—*At a Roman meet. Note general use of snaffle and loose running martingale.*

Constraint versus Comfort

So much with regard to jumping. As, however, riding, and even hunting or steeplechasing, do not consist in jumping only, let us examine the Italian seat under the aspect of long hours in the saddle not necessarily or continuously at the faster paces.

To the civilian anything even distantly connected with armies seems to convey an idea of perpetual and unflinching tenseness. I prefer attributing to this prejudice, rather than to any failure of mine clearly to elucidate a method by now three-score years old, the impression that seems to reign in a great many quarters as to the constraint which must be part of it. One correspondent—franker perhaps than most—writes me without much beating about the bush that he prefers lolling in the saddle; against declarations of independence such as these I admit having no valid arguments!

That the proper Italian position must make one "look alive" I would not deny if I could; in this sense, if you will, it is military and moreover typically "cavalry," and as nowadays the true sporting outdoor horse and the military horse are practically one, as they must both constitute fast, game, enduring and docile conveyances across a country, military and sporting equitation are basically one and the same thing: hence the military and sporting (cross-country) seat or position or balance—call it what you will—should in our day be identical, just as there should be no difference of actual shape between military and sporting saddles.

As to the strain that the Italian position is supposed to impose, Plate 22, in which both man and horse are in an attitude of relaxation, nevertheless shows the former—a Tor di Quinto instructor, by the way—in the perched attitude typical of the School. Even in the most violently active phases of riding there is, however, not much more tension on the part of the rider than this; there is on the other hand abundant store of reserve power in every part of the horseman's anatomy, which comes into play when necessary to create momentary tension of arm or leg or back. As in all games and sports correctly executed, *attention*—without strain—should be continuous, but *tension* only momentary, otherwise they become unbearably fatiguing. I have ever failed to

PLATE 30.—*American hunting seat.*

PLATE 31.—*Italian hunting seat.*

understand why it should be so difficult to convey, even to such as have never seen first-class Italian riding, that, naturally, our particular style of horsemanship is not an exception to the fundamental rule of alternating relaxation and tension, without which the correct execution of any sporting accomplishment is out of the question.

It has also been put forward that it is impossible to keep the correct Italian position except with free striding horses that are keen and take something of a hold, and that with a not very willing horse possessing a very light mouth it is necessary to relapse into the saddle, because, as he is behind the bit, he does not give the degree of contact indispensable to keeping a real forward position at fast paces.

Without at the present juncture going into a disquisition on bitting and schooling which would take us too far afield, I have already said that the horse that will not normally meet his bit is the rare exception and that most do so as a result of excessive bending and flexing. Furthermore, as it is customary to describe seat as a mixture of grip and balance, to render this definition really accurate we must qualify both its factors.

In the first place I do not fancy the word "grip" because it suggests a continuous rigid effort of the muscles of the thigh, whereas we have seen that our hold on the saddle should be *the mechanical automatic result on the knee of a given position of foot and ankle.*

As to balance, it is generally envisaged, I think, as purely lateral equilibrium, whereas in our particular case the forward diagonals A-AI and B-BI of Diagram C are what mainly concern us; it is only when we have sensed its right degree in relation to gravity that our hands become absolutely independent of our seat. It is therefore not our hold on the reins, but the inclination of the torso from the hip-joint and its corresponding forward poise with weight placed in the direction of these diagonals that enable us to maintain a forward position very similar to the ski balance and based on much the same principles of equilibrium and elasticity of angles.

It cannot be denied that, like every other worthwhile accomplishment, the correct poise is not easy to acquire by people past their prime who have ridden for years in a more happy-go-lucky way, but, if taken up reasonably early in life, it can be learnt and successfully practised, is

"Open Jumping."

also true. For instance, to most Europeans squatting on the heels would be a painful punishment, whereas Orientals, who have done it all their lives, sit thus in perfect ease for many a dreamy hour—by which I mean to convey that it all boils down to a question of habit, and that there cannot therefore be any plausible excuse for the round back, and the straight foot, the "wrapped" position of the leg, and arms bent almost double of the various avowed or unconfessed imitators of the Italian school. Although in some rare cases the failure, for example, to flex the ankle may be due to defective individual conformation, as a general rule it is the result of insufficient initial effort—or boots too tight in that particular place, a very frequent defect.

"Lightening the Forehand"

While on the subject of the various objections to forward riding in general and to the Italian version in particular, let us also analyze the all-too-prevalent credence that by lying back at jumps the rider lightens his mount's forehand and thereby prevents his overbalancing, decreasing at the same time the shock of landing.

A friend of mine suffered terrible injury in a motor collision because of the habit of stretching his legs straight out in front of him to brace himself. The thigh-bones were driven inwards by the force of an impact the consequence of which no other attitude could possibly have rendered so severe. As, mechanically speaking, the position of the legs of the jockeys in Plate 13 is the same, let us visualize the one at the top of the fence as my friend just before the collision, the horse as his car, the stirrup as that part against which he braced his feet and the ground as the opposing machine. Would not both the shock of collision and that of landing over Becher's [Brook is a fence jumped during the Grand National, a National Hunt horse race held annually at Aintree Racecourse near Liverpool, England. It is jumped twice during the race, as the sixth and 22nd fence, as well as on four other occasions during the year. It has always been a notorious and controversial obstacle, because of the size and angle of the 6 ft. 9 in. drop on the landing side. — *Editor's note.*] have been lighter if instead of keeping straight rigid legs both my friend and the jockey in question had bent their knees and thereby absorbed shock in their various joints?

As to the backward position preventing a horse overbalancing, it is on the contrary evident that this result is best attained—as I have repeatedly stated—by allowing the horse's trajectory to stretch freely, which is precisely what lying back and hanging on to the reins prevents. If the horse is obliged to take off with the whole weight of the rider mercilessly holding him back (Plate 24), it is clear that he will have to land at a more precipitous angle than if he were allowed to take off as in Plate 23—a comparison particularly interesting because both photographs are of precisely the same type of steeplechase jump, both obviously negotiated at racing pace. Which of the horses is having the better time it is not difficult to see.

Mannerisms

As I have often said, the Italian seat, conceived as the antithesis of the indoor equitation in vogue on the European continent and in its armies at the beginning of the present century, is *par excellence* not only a jumping but an outdoor seat. The exaggerations which followed after the disappearance of its creator from the human stage can be ascribed above all to the show-ring, and particularly to such competitions as involved or were entirely based on high jumping—and by exaggerations I do not allude solely to such as concern the actual seat, but also and particularly to the mania that developed at one time for excessive steadying of horses at their jumps to the detriment of the practical aspect of a system primarily meant not only as a safe but also a rapid conveyance in the open.

This sort of thing constituted a passing phase which, perhaps, lasted long enough still further to confirm our unfortunate reputation for unpractical riding, still occasionally thrown in our teeth in spite of the fact that even in show-ring jumping competitions—most of which now exact speed besides precision—the courses are often covered at racing pace.

The wholesome reaction against jumping purely for jumping's sake which, furthermore, seems to have set in, and the most promising sign of which is the increase of steeplechases and "cross-countries" our Cavalry

School pupils are obliged to take part in, added to the prolongation from three to six months of the Tor di Quinto complementary course, is already showing good results. To no one more than the writer has this change of direction given greater pleasure or been more a matter for congratulation, for whatever the defenders of the show-ring may say, jumping contests can easily fall, if they have not fallen already, from the equestrian pedestal to the level of super-specialized athletics.

IV: THE FLAT
Its Teachings

IT is not only in jumping that a horse can unwittingly but actively be interfered with: a wide and most instructive field for the study of certain problems is the comparatively uneventful flat.

I think few people—even among such as should in their professional interest do so—take the trouble carefully to observe jockeys' seats, or positions as it is more accurate to call them. When, for instance, a new star appears on the racing horizon, no matter how much public and Press may acclaim him, no attempt is ever made to analyze even the most evident elements directly responsible for his triumphs. American ideas with regard to flat-race riding invaded Europe three decades ago, and most of us have taken it for granted that the last word was said then and that it had once for all not only been accepted but understood. We are, on the contrary, labouring in this respect very much under the same sort of delusion that I have been at pains to explain and combat with regard to the Italian method.

Whether they themselves were personally ever aware of it or not, the success of the first American jockeys and of their particular system was due to the fact that what was then scathingly termed the "monkey seat" allowed a closer fusion of two centres of gravity—the man's and the horse's—than had ever been achieved before. This, added to a lesser resistance to air that the less upright position of the body engendered, resulted in the increase of speed that astounded the racing world of that day.

The new seat rapidly spread, to the chagrin of the dogmatically conservative jockeys and trainers in Europe, much as the Italian seat has spread and is spreading, although more slowly, and under various aliases, in other quite as orthodox equestrian fields. Like the Italian, however, the American seat has been distorted, and its basic principles almost lost sight of; but whereas the latter never was properly interpreted abroad, the original standard of the former in Europe has gradually deteriorated beyond recognition for lack of study and attention.

Plates 26 and 27, representing respectively an American and an English field, are chosen among hundreds which could just as conclusively be produced to bear out this same statement.

The gallop might be described as a series of incomplete falls, for a horse at this pace throws his centre of gravity forward at every stride and rejoins it just in time not to end on his nose (see fourth horse of Plate 27). The greater his speed, the longer his action must be to catch up, so to speak, with the centre of gravity he has thrown ahead. If, therefore, there is a case where a man should as much as possible vigorously but smoothly precede his mount it is precisely in a flat race and particularly at its finish. Nevertheless this is so little understood in Europe that there is hardly one jockey in a thousand that does not separate his centre of gravity from the horse's, especially in the agitation of a hard-ridden finish.

Not so his American colleague, who rides the whole race absolutely in the same position, literally glued flat to the horse, arms horizontally forward (Plate 26).

Flat races are ridden "all out" nowadays, generally over comparatively short distances. Whether this, added to much two-year-old racing, is good or bad for the future generations of the thoroughbred is not a question we have to deal with here. The fact remains that if in the old days—and not so very old at that—it was correct to begin slowly, and tentatively sparring for lead or place was a part of racing technique,[11] on modern courses, on the contrary, we generally see pace from start to finish; this does not, as might be supposed, by any means necessarily exclude science in race riding, for manoeuvring being, as a direct consequence, done at a much more rapid rhythm, it exacts sharper sensibilities and an infinitely more subtle sense of pace, for the greater the speed at which we travel the more important infinitesimal shadings become.

Why are most European jockeys apparently unable to move with their horses, and limit themselves more or less agitatedly to following them?

---

11   A friend once told me that he remembered as a small boy seeing Archer, Fordham and a third jockey whose name escapes me, peacefully chatting among themselves at the beginning of a race at Ascot!

PLATE 32.—*Example of deliberate reliance on reins for preservation of seat and balance*

PLATE 33.—*Example of deliberate reliance on reins for preservation of seat and balance*

I remember some years ago a race at Longchamp being lost so clearly by the jockey's being behind his horse, that I felt really sorry for the latter, it seemed so unfair. If memory serves it was one of the very long races so popular in France—the Arc de Triomphe over six thousand metres, I think—and if at the end the jockey was pumped he "came by it honest," but if he really had been riding properly he would not, even in his condition, have interfered with the horse's action to the extent of the head that lost him the race.

Although I hold no special brief for American horsemanship in the abstract, in the specific case of race-riding there is no doubt that Americans are, on the flat, infinitely superior to Europeans, and better than the English over obstacles. The characteristics of young countries being above all speed, America has for many years past taught the older countries how to "get there" first in many fields and not always at the expense of style. Other adolescent nations like South America, Australia, South Africa, etc.—to say nothing of the Far East —have in race-riding held more to the elder sister than to the ancient parent, having realized—probably unconsciously— the full importance of that inch which, though not as good as a mile, can easily develop into a length.

School for Jockeys

Perhaps some day an academy or university for jockeys will be founded, like the bull-fighters' universities of Spain, where apprentices will be really taught their profession not only practically but theoretically by qualified teachers, and not left, as they are at present, to pick up what they can as they go along either from older colleagues or trainers—many of them (be it said without offence) men whose wide practical experience is uncorroborated by the very important test of logical reasoning.[12] When we stop to consider that even horsemen of much higher social categories labour for years under incredibly mistaken impressions with regard to the mechanics and ballistics of the most elementary principles of riding, it is not surprising if others who, as a general rule, come from the less educated classes, are unable to reason out ways and means for their own and others' enlightenment. The professional jockey therefore remains mentally more

12   The above chapter was written long before the question of a school for jockeys was brought up in the public press by a well-known British horseman, since deceased.

A Study in Hand Positions.

or less where his environment and his direct superiors—trainers and senior jockeys—put him; his improvement is largely a matter of experience by reiteration rather than thoughtful experiment. I am willing to wager that not one in ten of the present—or past —successful jockeys would be able to explain with any degree of lucidity why he wins more races than his colleagues.

However, as environment must remain for the present the only deciding factor of the bent to be given budding jockeys, it stands to reason that the latter take and keep the orthodox stamp of their different nationalities, or rather continents (to preserve the differentiation already made between Europe and North or South America, Australia, South Africa, etc.).

Among the many unsatisfied aspirations that I am fairly certain to take with me to a not-too-early grave there will be, besides the pleasure of seeing a Grand National ridden according to my theories and convictions, the satisfaction of proving by practical test the inferiority of European flat-race jockeys. As circumstances prevent direct experiments which would run into more money than the writing of books on equitation brings in the present incarnation, I have to be content with the purer joys of the mind; I nevertheless maintain that, everything else (horses, of course, included) being equal, a jockey who has a clear idea and conception not only of the forward *seat* but of the forward *impulse* as applied to his profession, will beat another who "pushes" his horse and has neither the wit nor the intuition to see that he must avoid drawing his centre of gravity *away* from that of his mount. I am inclined to believe that position and forward impulse are the greater part of the game, for, although they are not in themselves enough to make a superlatively good jockey, they possibly represent 60 per cent, of the elements of success, the other forty being made up by the right physique, sense of pace, courage, quickness of decision, steady but rapidly reacting nerves, strength—of the supple not muscle-bound variety—the readiness to take a chance and judge of its ultimate possibilities, etc., etc.

Incidentally (this I know will be considered a particularly daring statement), slightly longer leathers which would allow them really to get more forward, and ride more with their knees, would do jockeys the world over no harm.

My complete jockey I have so far seen only in dreams, and not European dreams at that.

V: POLO AND THE ITALIAN METHOD

MUCH can be forgiven polo, for the verb "to play," applicable to games, not sports, absolves it by its very essence of sins it would otherwise be hard to condone; this is, however, insufficient reason for not at least attempting to eliminate as many of its shortcomings as possible for the sake of the animal without which there would be no polo, now inconsiderately regarded merely as a means to an immediate end by the fraternity of the long bit, high hand and ready heel.

Although there are many treatises on polo as a game, instruction in polo horsemanship is practically limited to such negative advice as that a roomy saddle, in which one can move about, be chosen because of comfort to an indifferent horseman, and that in selecting bridles one should buy such as accomplish their purpose with as little pain as possible. (I am quoting a great polo authority.) Why not, on the contrary, attempt to make the horseman a little less indifferent in more senses than one, and not merely teach him to fall back on a roomy saddle for his comfort? And, above all, why admit such unsound tenets as that of inevitable pain for the horse?

Leslie Cheape

Consider the photograph reproduced in Plate 34. Years ago it started a train of thought which I have never till recently attempted to follow to any conclusion, for the good reason that when polo in Italy was practically unknown, to contemplate Italian methods in relation to it would have been idle; all possibility of direct and convincing experiment to prove its potentialities, when the game remained limited to nations of the Anglo-Saxon type of horsemanship, was non-existent—especially as Leslie Cheape was dead.

Now, however, that polo—thanks to a few enterprising spirits—has been revived in my country, this picture has a direct bearing on theories until recently neglected but which are at present being studied in connection with certain technical aspects of the game.

Cheape's position is different from any English or American player's of note either of his time or any other; that it is the posture of a player considered, twenty years ago, the best in the world is a point of vital importance for our purposes, for if we simply imagine him seated four or five inches further forward without shifting the foot from its present place or in any way altering any other detail of his delightfully light and alert position—the attitude of his left hand not excluded—we get a pretty accurate imitation of Diagram A. Captain Cheape is therefore posthumously deposing in favour of a seat and system of which in polo he must have been knowingly or unwittingly the first and only English exponent. Thus sponsored, forward principles could almost pretend, on this recommendation alone, to the invasion of one of the last strongholds of haphazard riding—the polo ground.

Polo in Italy

I have said that polo has been revived in Italy, for it really had made a first, if meteoric appearance, thirty years ago.

Started in Rome on an unpretentious scale by a small group of foreign and native sportsmen, its existence then was brief, owing mainly to the fact that the foreigners, better and more expensively mounted on imported animals, outclassed and discouraged the local element on their *campagna* [countryside] ponies.

Buried at the time with but few tears, the game was resuscitated of recent years at Brioni and became one of the chief attractions of this charming island resort. The sporting commander of an Italian cavalry regiment next appeared on the scene by allowing his officers the use of troop horses for games which pleasantly occupied the idle hours of a small garrison town—but, promptly frowned upon by army authorities, polo's military career in Italy at this period was almost as brief as its

PLATE 34.—*A Forerunner—Leslie Cheape.*

civilian appearance before the war. It was left to the capital—Rome—to make another and really vigorous effort towards its recognition. The Roma Polo Club,[13] after a period of struggles and vicissitudes, finally took up its permanent residence on the left bank of the Tiber—opposite the Cavalry School on the right—and the game has definitely taken its place in the sporting and social life of Rome; that it has finally done so in the teeth of serious opposition makes its victory particularly interesting when we examine the reasons that came near closing Italian doors in its face.

Expensive as the game undoubtedly is, objections to polo were not so much of a material as of a technical order.

Only the very unobservant or the deliberately blind can possibly deny that most polo players are not good horsemen; some of the very best, although dashing riders, are very poor horsemen indeed, whose heedless violence of hands and weight on horses' loins abuse every single principle of the Italian method—that smooth, subtle and considerate *sistema* which its exponents have been and are at pains to preserve unsullied and unalloyed.

Polo's greatest enemy in Italy was therefore quite naturally the very element that, in others, is its most important pillar, i.e. the military, who saw in it the desecration of every principle of correct horsemanship—an attitude at first sight more than justified, not only because of the loose type of seat that English and Americans favour and seem to consider a *sine qua non* of the game, but principally with regard to the horse's head and neck in relation to the rider's hand, to the combined action of powerful bit and standing martingale tearing the jaws apart (Plate 37), the sharp turning on the quarters and other features barbarous in Italian cavalry eyes.

Thanks however to the persistent efforts of such as fancied the pastime (practically all civilians with little or no cavalry standards to safeguard), the game gradually overcame opposition, and the supple Italian mind has taken the problems of polo to heart and in conclusion

---

13   To Count Giacomo Antonelli, retired Cavalry Colonel and erstwhile Tor di Quinto instructor, is largely due the present movement in favour of polo in Italy. His efforts to introduce the game officially into the Italian Army have resulted in a group of Cavalry officers being sent to attend a special instruction course at Brioni, Count Antonelli is President of the Roma Polo Club.

accepted it, provided it becomes Italianized—a metamorphosis difficult to conceive, but perhaps not impossible of actuation.

Defects and Remedies

A point of the greatest importance is the Italian conception of turning; pulling up with a jerk and spinning around is considered a highly empirical way of attaining this object. A galloping horse, stopping suddenly, does not do so by throwing his head up but by putting it down. In spite of the originality of the rider's attitude this is what the pony in the foreground of Plate 36 is doing while turning, in a position of *balancier* evidently not made possible by any forethought on the part of the man on his back, but because, being apparently in a snaffle, the pony has been able to get the best of the player's hand—without the pain that in the case of the usual bit would have forced him to sit on his hocks.

Independently of the fact that a horse should never be arrested on the ewe-neck principle—who wants a ewe-necked horse? Are we quite sure that in polo there is always reason for the continual pivoting we indulge in? And doesn't the need for so much of it exist perhaps largely in our minds, together with the innumerable other stock ideas, not founded on fact, with which horsemen's mentalities are so astonishingly littered? I suggest the point be both theoretically and practically dissected, for it is no unusual sight to see a player pull his pony brutally on to its haunches, especially after missing the ball, turn briskly around and remain, stick in air, with absolutely nothing to do and nowhere in particular to go for a very much longer time than it would have taken him to turn more scientifically and less painfully. If polo were played one instead of four a side, stopping dead and turning on the haunches would evidently be indispensable, but if team work is what it should be cannot we leave the remedying of our mistakes and failures and their immediate consequences to our companions? That is, after all, what they are there for.

To pull the head up forcibly is harmful because in contrast with the horse's natural balance, resulting in unnecessary wear and tear on the horse's hocks, tendons and pasterns; furthermore, the evil effects on the bars are increased by the placing of the rider's weight nearer the loins than the withers, in the way typical of most perpendicular or backwardly inclined seats.

It is not so important, I think, that a horse turn in a small space as that he be quick after the ball and that he stop in as few strides as possible. For the former purpose, the freer his propelling apparatus, when needed to gallop on quickly, the better—obviously; for the latter, with time and patience it is not impossible to train ponies to the voice or pressure of the leg, or both, rather than attain the same ends by violence of hand and heel. (The voice to be effective should be sparingly used, for the incessant "whoas" some players indulge in end by being treated by the pony with the contempt familiarity engenders, and taken no notice of whatsoever!)

Hands and seat in polo, as in every other variety of riding, form a vicious circle; if we want them to be, as they always should, independent of each other, the only way is to rely on the hinge of the knees—and that alone—for the preservation of our position; to do this it is indispensable to rise in the saddle, heels down and body inclined forward; if we sit, our hinge automatically weakens, the knee loosens and the hand becomes less independent because hampered and interfered with by the shifting body.

Roughly, polo players' styles can be divided into four categories:

(a) Those who deliberately sit feet forward, in too close communion with the cantle of their saddles, through all the phases of the game, and believe that this is the best position in which to hit. This is perhaps the worst class, because they never give their ponies rest of mouth or back.

(b) Such as practise a mixed system by keeping on the stirrups galloping, and sitting down when they hit the ball, at the same time generally hauling at, instead of freeing, the horse's mouth.

(c) Such as reverse the foregoing and gallop sitting (Plate 40) perhaps on the principle that they are thereby pushing their mounts along, and stand in their stirrups to hit, generally taking a convenient tug at the horse's mouth to help them leave the saddle, and finally—

(d) The very few who, on the contrary, believe in standing in their stirrups and never sitting down—the forward riders, of whom the one in Plate 38 seems a fair example.

PLATE 35.—*Perfect swing from the hips.*

PLATE 36.—*Downward movement of horse's head in stopping.*

PLATE 37.—*The high and the low hand.*

In the light of even the most elementary logic I fail to perceive how (a), (b) and (c) can possibly be considered expedient ways of playing a game that requires speed, a steady seat and the utmost independence not only of hands but of the torso; nevertheless players, and good players, exist who do not yet see that the *(d)* position is the only one really adapted to the purpose, mixed systems as in every other form of horsemanship giving the poorest results. It is evident, as fortunately at least one first-class player sustains, that while standing in the stirrups the player is not affected by the gallop of his pony which he offsets by giving at the knees and ankles, the pony moving freely under him—which is also a position in which to hit a stronger and more accurate ball.

Perhaps categories (a), (b) and (c) are what we might call unconscious varieties of the genus polo-player, in the sense that they would probably not recognize their own portraits as above depicted because they are entirely unaware of the antics they go through in the stress and excitement of the game, and because they have never really given horsemanship, as such, a moment's thought.

In all fairness, I feel that I must qualify my assertion that polo players favour the high hand by adding that there is more excuse for it in polo than in any other form of riding. As the reins must perforce be held in one hand we have no choice but to run this up the horse's crest in giving him his head, whereas in the ordinary way the division of the reins between the two hands enables us to follow the horse's mouth without raising them—but if we can admit that the *advancing* hand at polo must perforce be raised (though not inevitably much above the horse's crest) the high *restraining* hand is nothing but a bad habit, the remedy for which is, obviously, to avoid as much as possible bringing the pony's head into anything but the natural position A-D of Diagram D; which brings the pressure of the bit in the right place—the bars and not the teeth or corners of the lips. Plate 37 shows both systems—the high and the low hand—and their mechanical results with respect to the ponies' heads. The upward jerk acts as shown in Plate 39, the raised poll reacting on the loins, pressed down besides by the rider's weight. To get some idea of how the pony must feel in these conditions the reader should get a friend to pull his head up with one hand under the

PLATE 38.—*Good forward position in polo.*

jaw, at the same time pressing with one knee hard on the small of the back! The only unconstrained angle of a horse's head in relation to the horizontal of the ground or the line of the spine is one of approximately 45 degrees (A-D, Diagram D) or slightly more. If we can go so far as to admit that exceptionally a horse's head may assume the perpendicular A-F it is inadmissible that it ever go, under any circumstances, to A-G, a posture much fancied for parade purposes, especially in the old days, but useless of its very essence.

Polo players turn their ponies by the touch of the reins on the side of the neck aided, theoretically at least, by leg pressure. Some advisedly raise and advance the hand to bring the reins to bear in a particularly sensitive place, the upper part of the neck near the ears—a trick common to rough-riders the world over. As, however, the reins should be kept always short and the hand forward but low, we ought to be able to turn by drawing it back, towards the groin, simultaneously twisting it from the wrist in either direction to signal our wishes to our pony, which, if

PLATE 39.—*The high hand in polo: Second, third and fourth ponies.*

PLATE 40.—*The seated position in polo: Evident strain on ponies' quarters in effort to gallop-on with weight on loins.*

properly trained, should, like all other well-schooled horses, respond to *indications* without it ever, or rarely, becoming necessary to develop them into *actions*.

Polo of the Future

I recommend the considerations contained in the present chapter to the attention of those concerned, with the prayer that thought be given to the suggestion of applying to their favourite game the mentality of modern methods. Rough-riding is every day less admired in civilized communities. Any effort that contributes to better finish in all branches of equitation should be welcomed with an open mind and not waved aside with the smirk of superiority—for often newcomers see things from unsuspected angles and find solutions that never occur to such as have their vision already dimmed by preconceived notions.

It is not enough for a horse to be well groomed and well fed or even conceded abundant rest; he, like a man, must be, above all, happy in his work. Good corn in the manger is insufficient recompense for aching loins, or the clearest water for bruised and bleeding bars. Discomfort and shock are, with care and intelligence, entirely avoidable; pain should only be inflicted as deliberate punishment, and that rarely. Both animals and men have a right to fair play and humane treatment. We must be able at any moment to realize with a clear conscience that we have nothing with which to reproach ourselves in our relations with the mute beast in our power, so that we may be justified in asking his maximum effort in our service, or, in grimmer games than polo, his very life in our cause.

I would that such positions as those of Plates 36, 37, 39 and 40 could be for ever suppressed and that horsemen would realize how often and how needlessly they abuse the laws of gravity, mechanics and anatomy.

I want to see all polo played some day in snaffles with no martingales of any description—by no means an impossibility, for I have seen it done, and done well. So long as even my own countrymen will continue to use severe bits and standing martingales in polo, which they now cannot help doing because still riding ponies schooled on the extant system, I shall feel that they are not entirely consistent with the principles of our great School.

I want to see the hand whenever possible held low, the jerk—fist up—and the pivoting on the quarters for ever relegated to the limbo of dead errors, or at least reduced to vanishing-point; above all, I want to see the immovable knee, the leg, from the knee down, in precisely the same place and position it should keep in jumping, the foot never lifted in that attitude apparently so dear to most polo-players (in my opinion unnecessary, incorrect and harmful because it loosens the seat), by which it almost reaches the level of the hip pocket. Furthermore, I want all swing of the body reduced to the turn of the torso pivoting from the hips (Plate 35).

These should be the features of modern polo riding which would make of the game—fascinating and exciting as it is— what its best friends cannot claim for it now—an interesting branch of the equestrian *art.*

VI: THE FORWARD SIDE-SADDLE

AN ungallant Italian riding-master of the late eighteenth century declared in no uncertain terms that the gentler sex was physically unadapted to riding. The early nineteenth century expressed horror at the mere idea of ladies riding astride; and as recently as 1910, a famous horsewoman described this position as an "incompetent and totally unsuitable style of riding for women." Be all this as it may, our sisters, mothers, wives and fiancées, continue to ride, both side and astride, and it is safe to assume that they will do so to the end of the chapter.

Although difference of build imposes certain reservations, where the cross-saddle is concerned what we say with regard to men applies with almost equal force to women; the sidesaddle demands a technique different in detail but not in essentials, for the correct principles of the forward seat are far from inapplicable, as I have frequently heard it sustained, to the female saddle.

The catchy phrase "forward seat" has struck the ear of modern saddlers, but "unfortunately it is generally built (the side-saddle) according to the fantastic ideas of fashionable makers who have no practical experience of side-saddle riding."[14] And what was true twenty-five years ago unfortunately still holds good. For example, one man of no mean reputation in his line says that the leaping pommel should be lower than it used to be and farther back, so as to bring the left leg to almost the same position "as when riding astride" (?), and that the whole seat being quite flat and not sloping downwards from withers to quarters enables the rider to adopt what is known as the forward seat, which he proceeds to describe as follows: "The grip used to be obtained by drawing back the left foot and then forcing the knee up under the leaping head. This made the wearing of a spur dangerous, as the heel was very likely to touch the horse's flank; also it put one in the very

---

14   Mrs. Hayes—*The Horsewoman*, 1910 (Third Edition).

worst possible position to resist the forward pull of a keen horse or of any horse when landing after a jump.

"Now get into your modern saddle. Sit well forward so that the pommel gets under the thigh, not under the knee; in this position your right leg will hang neatly down by the horse's shoulder, instead of the foot being somewhere on his neck, pointing skyward. You will find that your stirrup leather, to be comfortable, will be about three holes longer than with the old-fashioned saddle."

I agree with the "under the thigh and not under the knee" and with the advisability of the right leg hanging perpendicular to the ground, but I admit myself baffled when I am informed that the forward seat requires a longer leather than the old one. And where I really do protest, and that violently, is when I am further told that to get your grip, *you should straighten and stiffen* the left knee, which automatically brings the foot *forward*, not backward, and the left thigh hard against the leaping-head. "Press your right leg firmly against the horse's shoulder, drop your hands and there you are—in the best and most scientific position to resist any pull or propulsion you will ever get."

But where are you really after such scientific advice? "The modern forward seat is much less tiring for the horse, which carries his rider's weight in the place where it is most able to do so, namely, immediately behind the shoulder, instead of on the small of the back."

This sounds familiar, but it hardly tallies with the stiff leg and the forward foot, which are bound, on the contrary, to push the rider back. Let us recapitulate.

In the first place the forward position in the saddle must resemble its cross-saddle brother—or half-brother—and therefore all straight lines of leg must be taboo as detrimental to elasticity. The stiffened leg with the foot thrust forward may be a good position to resist pull or propulsion, but as the scientific controlling of a horse should in no way resemble a tug-of-war, there are other and better ways of attaining the same object. To this, as also to the necessity of resisting the forward pull on landing, which in other words is the horse's natural extension of the *balancier*, never to be interfered with, I would ask whoever tenders such advice to conjure up in his mind the consequences, both practical

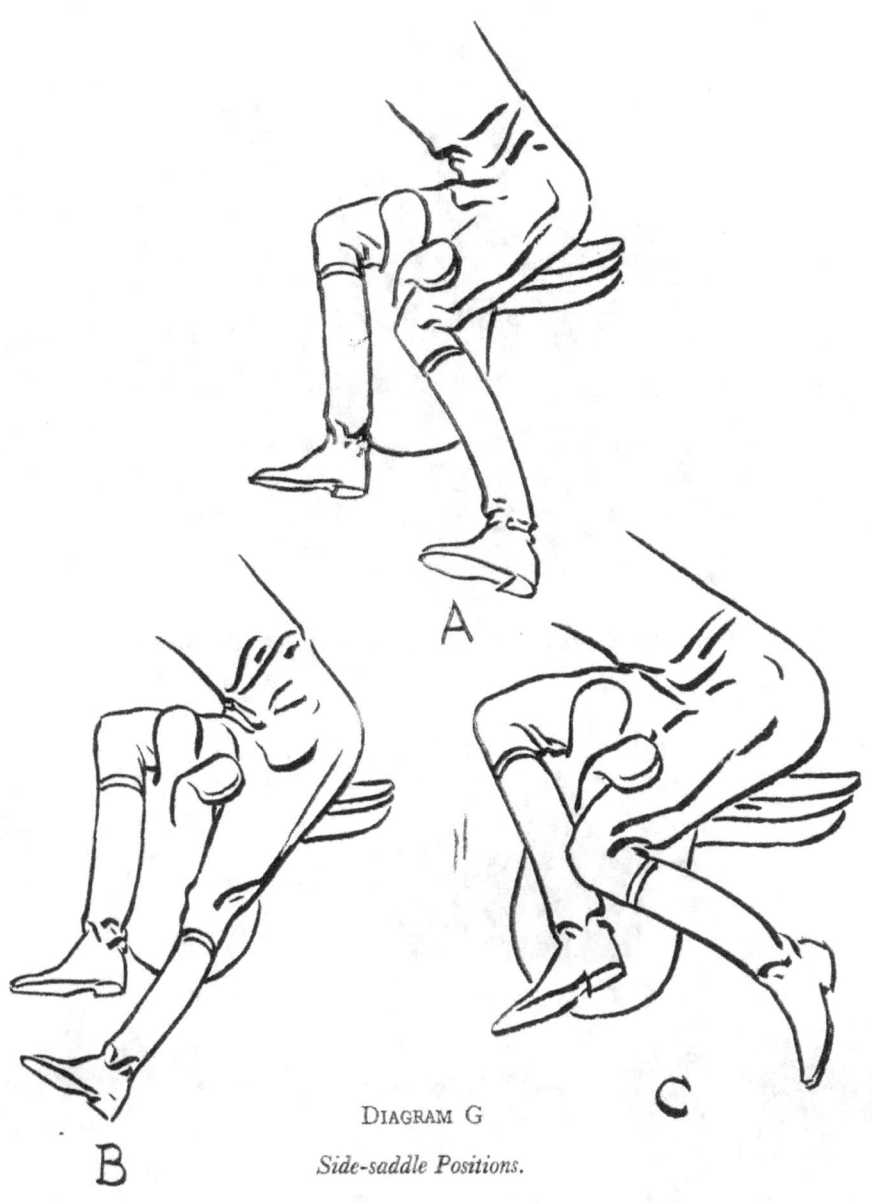

DIAGRAM G
Side-saddle Positions.

A—*Correct position.*
B—*Stiff left leg, foot forward.*
C—*Left foot swung back, "crushed" position of back.*

PLATE 41.—Écrasé *position inevitable with present side-saddle.*

PLATE 42.—*Excellent example of left leg and foot in correct position when jumping.*

and aesthetic, of applying the same principle to the male species, in which case the above phrase would read:

"Straighten and stiffen the knees, which will automatically bring the feet forward, etc."—a position, alas! all too often seen in practice, but never, I hope, deliberately taught even as a means of holding pulling horses or resisting propulsion.

As a matter of fact, the left leg on the side-saddle must be in the identical position of the leg in the cross-saddle, that is, the foot home in the stirrup, the heel down and the toe up, the foot turned as much as possible outward so as mechanically to force the knee against the saddle flap (Diagram G-A). The right leg from the knee down should hang perpendicularly, the body should be square, that is to say with the line of the shoulders at right angles to the horse's spine—a posture which automatically lightens the seat and, if correct, should leave only the right buttock really in the saddle, the other slightly out of it.[15]

In jumping, the left leg is not stiffened into one straight line and the foot stuck forward, but, as in the case of a man, loins, knees and ankles should act as shock absorbers (Diagram G-A). The stiff leg, on the contrary, reduces body and leg to one single angle or one straight line, both extremely hard on horse and rider, particularly in landing (Diagram G-B) whether the body is held straight, or back in the old-fashioned position, or bent forward either with rounded back, or the concave loins of the man's correct jumping position. It is almost better, if we are to choose between these evils, to let the leg swing back (Diagram G-C), a compromise less harmful in the side-saddle than in the cross because in the former there is at least the grip of the right leg around the upper crutch to counterbalance the resulting looseness. That the stiff leg is necessary to the avoidance of the horse's flank is absurd. If the foot is in the right position, behind the perpendicular of the knee (Diagram A, line A-B), heel down, toe up, either man or woman can wear three inches

---

15   "It is not sufficient in order to have a sure seat in the saddle for a woman to place her weight all on her right thigh. The secret of the square and graceful seat at all paces is for the woman so to seat herself in the saddle that her right thigh is parallel to the horse's backbone. This brings the shoulders around naturally without twisting and places the woman from the waist up—as well as her left leg—in approximately the same position as a man's. It means however that her left buttock is practically out of the saddle altogether." Lida L. Fleitmann—"Comments on Hacks and Hunters."

of steel with safety. At the beginning of the Great War, very short spurs not being fashionable and drop spurs not invented, most cavalrymen were heeled like game-cocks—and heeled high— and although sharp rowels were still at that time much in evidence, horses not only were not disembowelled, but even greys did not invariably show gory flanks. It is certainly not, therefore, to save the horse or avoid danger that a stiff knee becomes inevitable in either mode of riding.

There is perhaps one point on which it is particularly difficult, with the present saddles, for a woman to interpret the forward seat like a man—and that is in respect to rising out of the saddle. This is already hard to do when galloping, owing to the one stirrup of the side-saddle as against the two of the cross-saddle; it becomes doubly arduous during the impulse necessary to the clearing of obstacles, on account of the present leaping-head that effectually prevents any rising in the saddle by the breadth of its contact with the thigh. A woman therefore is perforce more seated than a man and must willy-nilly adopt in jumping a somewhat *écrasé* [Editor's note: "crushed"] position of the body (Plate 41), instead of rising in the irons like a man—who has nothing to hinder the free advance of his thighs.

A woman's left thigh having to be more in contact with the leaping-head with the shorter leather required by the forward position as we interpret it, posting at the trot might present one more difficulty to the many that result from a woman's not being able to rise freely. A return to the older fashioned narrow leaping-head, which has been of late years discarded without any cogent reason, would, I hold, be the solution of both the above problems. A leaping-head which would occupy a lesser surface would leave greater freedom of action in the vertical direction than the one now in such general use. It is true that with the former type of pommels, especially if the two are close together, the rider gets less assistance, but as in a good cause difficulties are not meant to be avoided but overcome, the subject is worthy the study and effort that will bring technically correct results. The *seated* forward position, let us remember, bears at best the bar sinister of a makeshift and of a problem half solved; let us therefore examine the possibilities of a more satisfying version.

Side-saddles vary according to their makers much more than men's, and though at given periods they have on general lines followed certain

Disorder.

fashions, there is now a somewhat regrettable lack of standardization, due perhaps to what might be called the present epoch of transition which is affecting both male and female riding, the new not having completely conquered the old, and what the former really consists in being far from clear to most people's minds.

The main characteristic of the *dernier cri* [trend] in women's saddles, and a feature common to almost all modern makers, is the absolutely straight and very long seat which is supposed to facilitate the forward position—another statement I beg leave to query.

Following the principle of the man's forward saddle, the seat not only should not be flat but concave. This curve, provided of course it is correct and the saddle properly fitted and not set sloping back from the withers in the direction of the loins, favours the forward position by automatically placing the rider nearer the pommel owing precisely to the swing of the seat.

In conclusion, the forward seat side-saddle should possess the following characteristics:

    1—Concave seat—shorter than the present one.
    2—Narrow leaping-head.
    3—The pommels not too wide apart.
    4—The leather hung perhaps slightly farther back to facilitate the preservation of the ankle-, knee-, hip-joint angles.
    5—Greater lightness.

The left leg should be in the same position as riding astride, for the mechanics ought to be identical, even if one-sided.

All of which leads to a paradoxical corollary: this branch of riding has regressed by progressing, for the old-fashioned saddle, which to a great degree possessed the above enumerated characteristics, would be better adapted to the modern forward seat than those now specially built for the purpose.

VII: ON STYLE, BEAUTY AND TAILORS

STYLE is much more than appearance; it goes deeper than mere looks, and—as the late Count Görtz used to say—is more important than victory.

To obtain the most out of any exercise we must begin by freeing its component parts of all parasitical superfluities and proceed by severe training of mind and body to further reduce the quintessence left by this wasting process to its highest and most subtle expression: in other words, through our nervous sensibility, we draw matter as close as possible to the spirit.

The basis of good fencing is to constrict within the narrowest limits the circle of the sword's point play. Time and space being inseparable, it stands to reason that the nearer the point, and therefore the blade, keep to direct and straight lines of attack and defence the quicker and more effective will sword play be.

The same applies to any game of agility and strength. The rhythm and accuracy which cause the acrobat to swing safely from one trapeze to another at giddy heights is the result of style—motion in its simplest expression. A pugilist I greatly admired, succeeded, in spite of a frail physique, in the most brilliant of careers, because, by reducing his movements to an elusive minimum, he had developed a style of inexorable precision.

An expert has carefully diagnosed the various elements which in his opinion go to the making of a tennis champion. For a player to give of his best and highest he should, according to this critic, possess:

20 per cent, physical aptitudes (athletic qualities),

30 per cent, special aptitude for that particular game (prompt reflexes, character),

50 per cent, style.

I commend the above proportions to the attention of such as persist in believing in the natural horseman instead of the natural horse, adding that for equitation I personally would be inclined to modify the above formula as follows:

20 per cent, physical aptitude,
20 per cent, special aptitude,
60 per cent, style (acquired).

Furthermore, if fine feathers do not make fine birds, smooth feathers certainly accompany orderliness of mind and soul.

We have been speaking of technique and style and of their correlation, and trying to analyze causes and effects. Trimness we have established beyond possibility of contradiction as indispensable to efficiency of style; trimness of attitude and movement go hand in hand with orderliness of apparel.

Modern man wears clothes—and it is very important that riding clothes follow the severity of our perhaps dearly acquired style. I am far from signifying that a horseman should ever resemble an undertaker in somberness, for one of the few sartorial pleasures left us in an unpicturesque age—and of which we should take full but judicious advantage—is precisely that of being able to wear more colourful apparel than custom allows for the ordinary activities of life—but the usual sense of measure that we should try to develop, if it does not happen to be part of our nature, should keep us within reasonable limits and help us kindly but firmly to discourage such sporting tailors as seem to have taken "Louder and Funnier" for their motto.

Apart from line and colour and a general sense of the fitness of things which should instinctively prevent our wearing, for example, brown boots with pink, or shepherd's plaid breeches with tops (combinations I have seen with my own eyes), the main characteristic we should strive for is to have every part of our kit in place. Form will suffer severely by a tie flying freely in the breeze, or by a spur hanging loosely to the heel and bobbing up and down with every movement. Spurs, incidentally, should always be worn with boots which, without, look about as smart as evening shirts without ties.

The days of fluttering ribbons and elaborate furbelows are past; they have gone with the *courbette,* the powdered wig and the long, rowelled spur. The stock has taken the place of the jabot of priceless lace, and even the long thin veil that floated from the little tip-tilted hats of our grandmothers retired long ago to perennial rest in the bottom of some old trunk in the attic. Sporting silhouettes, both male and female, are reduced to their most workmanlike expression—which should not be a matter of too much regret, for to keep alive the memory and the spirit of a truly sporting epoch, the early eighteen-hundreds have left us their orange-peel waistcoats, their gold buttons, the scarlet and the shad-bellies of their day with which to make a brave show behind the Master on the mornings when a southerly wind and a cloudy sky fill our hearts with the hope, and then perhaps the joy, of "forty minutes on the grass without a check."

APPENDIX A

THE following list is as complete as it has been possible to make it, although there may be other omissions besides those of the names of two or three other Spanish officers whose names I fail to recall. My apologies are due to them or any others I may not have brought to memory or have not found in the records of the Cavalry School.

For the information of those not familiar with the organization of the Italian Cavalry School I add that Pinerolo, near Turin, is the older school to which student officers are sent before they go to Tor di Quinto, near Rome, for a finishing course consisting almost entirely of cross-country work, obligatory hunting with the Rome Fox Hounds, and steeplechasing during the months of January, February and March.

The foreign officers who come to the Cavalry School follow either both or one of the courses.

The institution of Tor di Quinto as a military school of equitation is due, oddly enough, to a civilian sportsman, Marchese Luciano di Roccagiovine, for many years (1895-1907) Master of the Rome Fox Hounds, who was the first to realize the value practical experience of cross-country riding in the Roman *campagna* [countryside] could have for the young cavalry officers, as the finishing touch to their riding education.

Roll of Foreign Officers, graduates of the Italian Cavalry School of Pinerolo and Tor di Quinto, from the inception of the Caprilli Era to 1934, through whom the principles of the Italian Method of Equitation have spread to all the armies of the world.

PINEROLO

ARMY	NAME OF OFFICER	YEAR
Montenegrin	LT. M. TOMANOVITCH	1900-1901
Russian	LT. P. RODZANKO[16]	1906-1907
Spanish	LT. GARCIA-ASTRAIN	1906-1907
Spanish	LT. BOCETA	1906-1907
Spanish	LT. CHACEL[17]	1910-1911
Greek	LT. D. PAPPADIAMANTOPULO	1910-1911
Swedish	CAPT. HAMILTON	1920-1921
Swedish	CAPT. G. PEJRON	1920-1921
Polish	S.-LT. ZAWIZZA	1920-1921
Polish	LT.-COL. S. ZAHORSKI	1920-1921
Finnish	CAPT. SODESTROM	1920-1921
Danish	H.R.H. PRINCE VIGO OF DENMARK	1920-1921
Danish	LT. E. HEDMENN	1920-1921

16. Lieutenant, now Colonel, Paul Rodzanko returned to Russia to instruct in the Italian Method at the Imperial Cavalry School and organized the Horse Show Team which was the sensation of the Olympia (London) and Madison Square (New York) shows in 1914. Driven from his country by the revolution, he has taught equitation in England and was for an all-too-brief period instructor at the Irish Free State Cavalry School. It is indisputably due to its adoption of Colonel Rodzanko's Italian principles that the Irish Free State Horse Show Team has of recent years taken a foremost place in international competitions.

17. These three Spanish officers were eventually chosen by the Madrid Cavalry School to study the transformation of its system of instruction. The principles of the Italian School have since been adopted as the basis for the training and schooling of both horses and riders.

APPENDIX

ARMY	NAME OF OFFICER	YEAR
Norwegian	Lt. C. Guldberg	1920-1921
Swedish	Capt. de Rosembland	1920-1921
Swedish	Major Tannlum	1920-1921
Swedish	Lt. Wilkstrom	1920-1921
Finnish	Lt. de Kristierson	1920-1921
Finnish	Lt. G. de Haartman	1920-1921
Finnish	Lt. E. Avellan	1920-1921
Swedish	Lt. Brandstromm	1920-1921
Yugoslav	Lt.-Col. D. V. Pavlovitch	1920-1921
Yugoslav	Capt. R. Petrovitch	1920-1921
Yugoslav	Capt. U. Petruhar	1920-1920
Yugoslav	Capt. E. de Bona	1920-1921
Swiss	Capt. C. Huhn	1920-1921
British	Capt. Bowden Smith[18]	1920-1921
Swiss	Capt. Kuhn	1922
Swedish	Lt. Eckstrom	1923
Dutch	Capt. van de Steen	1923
Dutch	Capt. G. J. Rurinck	1923
Swedish	Lt. B. Sandstrom	1924-1925
Czekoslovak	Lt. R. Popler	1924-1925
Roumanian	Lt. A. Mitache	1924-1925
Peruvian	Major Vasquez Benavides	1924-1925
Peruvian	Major J. Silva	1924-1925
Spanish	Major della Marcorra y Carratalà	1924-1925
Dutch	Lt. G. de Kruyff	1925-1926
Mexican	Lt. M. Badillo	1925-1926
Turkish	Lt. Anni Effendi	1925-1926
Dutch	Capt. van Steembergen	1925-1926

18. At present and for some years past head of the British Cavalry School at Weedon.

APPENDIX

ARMY	NAME OF OFFICER	YEAR
Persian	Major Hessam	1925-1926
Persian	Lt. Nasratellah Khan Motazedi	1925-1926
Persian	S.Lt. Gemshid Khan Heydari	1925-1926
Swedish	Lt. F. Arne	1927
Turkish	Capt. Vehli Bey	1928-1929
Swedish	Lt. A. E. B. Flach	1928-1929
Mexican	Lt.-Col. S. Urbina	1928-1929
Mexican	Capt. Barriguete	1928-1929
Lithuanian	Lt. Autanas Andrianas	1928-1929
Lithuanian	Lt. Polivas Tyrullis	1928-1929
Swiss	Lt. A. Kadan	1928-1929
Equadorian	Major B. Valdiviesco	1928-1929
German	Capt. Count E. von Rothkirch und Trach[19]	1928-1929
Japanese	Major Yasushi Imamura	1929
Hungarian	Capt. A. Kanya	1929
Hungarian	Capt. D. Nemeth	1929
Hungarian	Capt. D. Reznek	1929
Hungarian	Lt. Imbre Bodò	1929
Swedish	Lt. Baron M. F. Barnekow	1929
Lithuanian	Lt. Juozas Ugianskis	1929
Mexican	Lt.-Col. S. Urbinas	1929
U.S.A.	Lt. E. T. Argo	1930
Portuguese	S.-Lt. J. G. de Gouveia Beltrao	1930
U.S.A.	Capt. J. Short	1930
Mexican	Capt. P. Orbs	1930

19. Of the Hanover Cavalry School. The comparatively recent successes of the German Army Horse Show Team, in consequence of a sudden and arresting improvement in their riding, is not difficult to trace, through this channel, to Italian influence.

APPENDIX

ARMY	NAME OF OFFICER	YEAR
U.S.A.	Capt. C. B. Cox	1931
U.S.A.	Capt. J. Watkins	1931
Albanian	Lt. U. Kurti	1931
Albanian	Lt. T. Verlaci	1931
Swiss	Lt. Muller	1931
Japanese	Lt. Munekatsu	1931
Swedish	Lt. Count B. A. Hamilton	1931
Dutch	Capt. H. Treffers	1931
Dutch	Lt. J. F. Greter	1931-1932
Ecuadorian	S.-Lt. C. G. Moncayo	1931-1932
Mexican	Lt.-Col. V. Peralta	1931-1932
Mexican	Major R. Orozco	1931-1932
Mexican	Capt. A. Villareal	1931-1932
Swiss	Major de Muralt[20]	1932-1933
Chinese	S.-Lt. Tam Sing	1932-1933
U.S.A.	Capt. C. C. Jadwin	1933
U.S.A.	Capt. G. Mitchell	1933
U.S.A.	Major T. G. Watkins	1932

TOR DI QUINTO

Greek	Lt. N. Vassas	1907-1908
Greek	Lt. C. Vassos	1907-1908
Bulgarian	Capt. G. Kissioff	1909-1910
Bulgarian	Lt. M. Mirkoff	1909-1910
Bulgarian	Lt. M. Zoribann	1909-1910
Roumanian	Lt. L. Balais	1910-1911

20. Member of the Swiss Army Horse Show Team on many occasions and one of the best known "internationals" in Europe.

ARMY	NAME OF OFFICER	YEAR
British	Lt. Dugdale	1911-1912
British	Capt. W. Nelson	1911-1912
Bulgarian	Capt. C. Donkeff	1911-1912
Bulgarian	Lt. W. Obreskoff	1911-1912
Roumanian	Lt. F. Jacob	1912-1913
Roumanian	Lt. Rachemberg	1912-1913
Swedish	Lt. F. Bennet	1912-1913
Bulgarian	Lt. F. Czenoff	1913-1914
Danish	H.R.H. Lt. Prince Vigo of Denmark	1921
Danish	Lt. H. Hedmann	1921
Polish	Lt.-Col. S. Zarorchi	1921
Japanese	Capt. Yamamoto Hiroschi	1921
Swedish	Lt. Brandstromm	1921
Finnish	Lt. de Kristierson	1921
U.S.A.	Major W. W. West, Jr.	1923
U.S.A.	Major H. D. Chamberlin[21]	1923
Yugoslav	Lt. Col. D. V. Pavlitch	1923
Yugoslav	Capt. R. Petrovitch	1923
Yugoslav	Capt. U. Petruhar	1923
Yugoslav	Capt. E. de Bona	1923
Swiss	Capt. C. Huhn	1923
Finnish	Capt. Suderstrom	1923
Peruvian	Major Vasquez Benavides	1926
Peruvian	Major J. Silva	1926
Swiss	Capt. Stoeffel	1926
Swedish	Lt. Dyrssen	1926
Persian	Major Hessam	1926
Persian	Lt. Nasratellah Khan Motazedi	1926
Persian	Lt. Gemshid Khan Heydari	1926
Mexican	Major M. Badillo	1927

21. Lt. Colonel Chamberlin needs no introduction to the American public.

APPENDIX

ARMY	NAME OF OFFICER	YEAR
Dutch	Capt. G. de Kruyff	1927
Turkish	Lt. Anni Effendi	1927
Swedish	Lt. F. Arne	1927
Swedish	Capt. N. Brunsen	1928
Swedish	Lt. A. E. B. Flach	1928
Swiss	Lt. A. Kaden	1928
U.S.A.	Capt. N. E. Fiske[22]	1929
Swedish	Lt. Baron M. F. Barnekow	1929
Swedish	Lt. A. E. B. Falk	1929
Turkish	Capt. Wekki Omar	1929
Lithuanian	Lt. A. Andrianas	1929
Hungarian	Capt. I. Bodò	1930
U.S.A.	Capt. J. C. Short	
Hungarian	Capt. D. Nemeth	1930
Hungarian	Capt. D. Reznek	1930
Hungarian	Capt. A. Kania	1930
Japanese	Major Yasushi Imamura	1930
Mexican	Lt.-Col. S. Urbinas	1930
Mexican	Capt. A. Barriguete	1930
Lithuanian	Capt. Ivozas Ugianskis	1931
Swedish	Lt. Count B. A. Hamilton	1931
Swiss	Capt. F. Muller	1931
Japanese	Lt. Munekatsu	1931
U.S.A.	Capt. C. B. Cox	1931
Albanian	S.-Lt. T. Verlaci	1932
Albanian	S.-Lt. A. Kurti	1932
U.S.A.	Capt. J. Watkins	1932
Ecuadorian	S.-Lt. G. Moncajo	1933

22. For some years instructor at the Philadelphia City Troop and recently United States Army Observer with the Italian forces in Ethiopia.

ARMY	NAME OF OFFICER	YEAR
U.S.A.	LZT]. G. MZITCHELL]	1933
U.S.A.	LZT]. C. C. JZADWIN]	1933
Swiss	MZAJOR] ZDE] MZURALT]	1933
British	CZAPT]. W. CZARR]	1934

APPENDIX B

THE version in English of the Regulations for the Equestrian Sports of the 1936 Olympiads, published in Berlin, which only came to my notice after the American edition of this book had been set up in type (July 1936), employs the word "collected" in the Special Rules for the Dressage Test of the Three-day Event.

Owing to my prolonged absence from Europe it has been impossible for me to secure a copy of these Rules in French, the official language of the Federation Equestre Internationale, but as the Italian rendering definitely and exclusively uses the word *"rallentato"* [Italian word: *rallentato* - definition is "slowed down." — *Editor's note.*] (Fr.: *-ralenti* [French word: *ralenti* - definition is "slow motion." — *Editor's note.*]) whenever "collected" is employed in the English text, I can only conclude that this contradiction is the result of defective or careless translation from French into English.

XENOPHON PRESS LIBRARY
www.XenophonPress.com

Xenophon Press is dedicated to the preservation of classical equestrian literature. We bring both new and old works to English-speaking riders.

30 Years with Master Nuno Oliveira, Henriquet 2011
A New Method to Dress Horses, Cavendish 2015
A Rider's Survival from Tyranny, de Kunffy 2012
Another Horsemanship, Racinet 1994
Art of the Lusitano, Yglesias de Oliveira 2012
Austrian Art of Riding, Poscharnigg 2015
Baucher and His School, Decarpentry 2011
Breaking and Riding, Fillis 2015
Classic Show Jumping: the de Nemethy Method, de Nemethy 2016
Divide and Conquer Books 1 & 2, Lemaire de Ruffieu 2016
Dressage in the French Tradition, Diogo de Bragança 2011
Dressage Principles Illuminated, Expanded Edition, de Kunffy 2016
École de Cavalerie Part II, Robichon de la Guérinière 1992, 2015
Equine Osteopathy: What the Horses Have Told Me, Giniaux 2014
François Baucher: The Man and His Method, Baucher/Nelson 2013
Great Horsewomen of the 19th Century in the Circus, Nelson 2015
Gymnastic Exercises for Horses Volume II, Russell 2013
H. Dv. 12 Cavalry Manual of Horsemanship, Reinhold 2014
Handbook of Jumping Essentials, Lemaire de Ruffieu 1997
Handbook of Riding Essentials, Lemaire de Ruffieu 2015
Healing Hands, Giniaux, DVM 1998
Horse Training: Outdoors and High School, Beudant 2014
Learning to Ride, Santini 2016
Legacy of Master Nuno Oliveira, Millham 2013
Methodical Dressage of the Riding Horse, Faverot de Kerbrech 2010
Principles of Dressage and Equitation, Fillis 2016
Racinet Explains Baucher, Racinet 1997
Science and Art of Riding in Lightness, Stodulka 2015

The Art of Riding a Horse or Description of Modern Manege,
    D'Eisenberg 2015
The Art of Traditional Dressage, Volume I DVD, de Kunffy 2013
The Ethics and Passions of Dressage Expanded Ed., de Kunffy 2013
The Forward Impulse, Santini 2016
The Gymnasium of the Horse, Steinbrecht 2011
The Horses, a novel, Elaine Walker 2015
The Italian Tradition of Equestrian Art, Tomassini 2014
The Maneige Royal, de Pluvinel 2010, 2015
The Portuguese School of Equestrian Art, de Oliveira/da Costa 2012
The Spanish Riding School & Piaffe and Passage, Decarpentry 2013
To Amaze the People with Pleasure and Delight, Walker 2015
Total Horsemanship, Racinet 1999
Training with Master Nuno Oliveira double DVD set, Russell 2016
Truth in the Teaching of Master Nuno Oliveira, Russell 2015
Wisdom of Master Nuno Oliveira, de Coux 2012

Available at www.XenophonPress.com

www.ingramcontent.com/pod-product-compliance
Lightning Source LLC
Chambersburg PA
CBHW050558300426
44112CB00013B/1982